Textile Surface Manipulation

stamen × 3½.
integrifolia
part of flowering plant × ⅔. B2 stamen × 1½.
style and ovary × 1½.

aculeata
inflorescence × ⅔.
style and ovary × 2. C3 stamen × 2.
part of fruiting stem × ⅔.

econopsis, so named from the Greek *mēkōn* 'py', *opsis* 'resemblance', has its centre of bution in the Himalaya and western China, about forty species mostly having blue, lish or yellow flowers. However, the type es is the European *M. cambrica*, the Welsh y (plate 11), the only one not found in the East. Perhaps the most famous of the Blue imalayan Poppies is *M. betonicifolia*, of h a variety with a hairy ovary was named *aileyi*; this last plant created a horticultu- tion after its introduction by F. Kingdon d in 1924. *M. nepaulensis* was the first Asi- es described botanically, being published in By 1896 botanical exploration had provid- ner twenty-two different species.

e popular horticultural plants are the bl- ered species such as the Himalayan Pop- *etonicifolia* and *M. grandis* but purity a- sity of colour often depend on soil a- ate. The yellow-flowered *M. dhwojii*, *rifolia*, *M. paniculata* and *M. regia* are also without beauty. Perhaps the most serious vantage about *Meconopsis* as garden plants at most species are monocarpic and so die flowering and fruiting only once.

nging from central Nepal, east through r Burma and into China, *M. horridula* (A) s at altitudes between 10,000 and 19,000 3050-5790 m.) with its uppermost recorded high on Mount Everest. It was so named in on account of its bristly nature, after being have erroneously been given specific names by botanists. It was introduced in 1904 and continues to show extreme variation even under the relatively uniform conditions of gardens. Luxuriant and dwarf plants sometimes growing side by side.

Discovered by N. Przewalski in Kansu in 1872, *M. integrifolia* (B) was initially placed in the genus *Cathcartia* by Maximowicz, in commemo- ration of James W. Cathcart (1802-1851), an amateur botanist and student of Himalayan flora. The species is found in alpine meadows and on screes in western China, upper Burma and Tibet, where it sometimes grows 5 to 3 feet (24 cm.) tall and may bear four or more flowers, although at its highest limits of growth, about 16,000 feet (4880 m.), the rosetted leaves may only have a solitary stalkless flower in its midst. The leaves may be up to 6 inches (15 cm.) long and 2 inches (5 cm.) broad, with an attractive covering of golden or brownish tufts. As well as the yellow flowered form, white and pink-flowered forms are known, the latter collected by Joseph Rock in 1932. The plant was originally introduced to cultivation in France in 1904 by Abbé Farges, while British gardens received seed from E. H. Wilson and Kingdon Ward in 1913. It has since been crossed with *M. betonicifolia* & *M. grandis* as *M. × sarsonsii*.

Found in Kashmir and the north-western Himalaya to Kumaon at altitudes between 10,000 and 14,000 feet (3050-4270 m.), *M. aculeata* (C) grows amongst rocks and scree streams. Hugh Francis Clarke Cleghorn (1820-1895) sent seed to Kew from north-west India and in 1864 it flowered for the first time in cultivation. It is not so widely grown as the larger and more intensely coloured species, such as *M. betonicifolia*.

Textile Surface Manipulation

Nigel Cheney &
Helen McAllister

HERBERT PRESS
LONDON · OXFORD · NEW YORK · NEW DELHI · SYDNEY

HERBERT PRESS
Bloomsbury Publishing Plc
50 Bedford Square, London, WC1B 3DP, UK
1385 Broadway, 5th Floor, New York, NY 10018

BLOOMSBURY, HERBERT PRESS and the Herbert Press logo are trademarks of Bloomsbury Publishing Plc

First published in Great Britain in 2013
This edition published in 2020

Copyright © Nigel Cheney and Helen McAllister, 2013

Nigel Cheney and Helen McAllister has asserted their right under the Copyright, Designs and Patents Act, 1988, to be identified as Author of this work

All rights reserved. No part of this publication may be reproduced or transmitted in any form or by any means, electronic or mechanical, including photocopying, recording, or any information storage or retrieval system, without prior permission in writing from the publishers

Bloomsbury Publishing Plc does not have any control over, or responsibility for, any third-party websites referred to or in this book. All internet addresses given in this book were correct at the time of going to press. The author and publisher regret any inconvenience caused if addresses have changed or sites have ceased to exist, but can accept no responsibility for any such changes

A catalogue record for this book is available from the British Library

Library of Congress Cataloguing-in-Publication data has been applied for

ISBN: 978-1-78994-039-8

2 4 6 8 10 9 7 5 3 1

Commissioning editor: Susan James
Assistant editor: Agnes Upshall
Copy editor: Jane Anson
Cover design: Eleanor Rose
Page layouts: Susan McIntyre

Printed and bound in India by Replika Press

To find out more about our authors and books visit www.bloomsbury.com and sign up for our newsletters

DISCLAIMER
Everything written in this book is to the best of our knowledge and every effort has been made to ensure accuracy and safety, but neither authors nor publisher can be held responsible for any resulting injury, damage or loss to either persons or property.

IMAGES
Front cover (clockwise from top): *Croquis* pattern design; Quilted coat back (photo by Philip White, model Polina Yakobson); Dip-dyed yarn used to create a dense garter-stitch structure; Samples exploring different pompom and stem constructions using a found twisted cord and a French knitted cord.

Back cover: Bias tape flower.

Frontispiece: Mood board inspired by *Meconopsis*.

Contents page (left to right): Knit pattern disrupted and broken to expose areas with pulled or dropped stitches; Parallel lines of spot stitches are worked over a knit structure to create a bobbly fabric; Close-up detail of running stitch.

Unless otherwise credited, all images are copyright of Nigel Cheney.

Contents

1 Introduction 7
2 Visual research 8
3 Repeat structures 26
4 Building surfaces: constructing or creating a fabric from scratch 33
   Working with soluble fabrics 33
   Detached buttonhole stitch 42
5 Decorating surfaces: embellishing an existing surface 46
   Working with imagery 46
   Working with an existing structure, grid or mesh 52
6 Manipulating: taking a surface and changing it through stitch 80
   Quilting 80
7 Deconstructing: taking a surface and disrupting it 98
   Changing surfaces 98
   Making holes with a soldering iron 98
   Distressing fabrics using an embellisher machine (electronic needle-felt) 103
8 Trims and edges 120
   Tassels 121
   Pompoms 126
   Buttons 135

Suppliers 137
Gallery 139
About the authors 141
Acknowledgements 143
Index 144

Nigel Cheney, 'Boxes I' from 'Goldilocks and the Bears' exhibition, Dalkey, 2011.

Introduction

1

This book is all about developing a diverse variety of textile techniques from personal visual inspiration, and applying these to specific projects. Projects could range from fashion to interior approaches, for a wide variety of customers. This encourages the exploration of an individual visual source to see its potential for imagery, texture, structure, and manipulation as a basis for sampling and design development in order to enthuse readers to create their own pieces. Within each project are hints on how to explore alternative possibilities to make the project unique. The creative potential that can be harnessed from the variety of images and notebook pages will be reinforced in each individual project. Techniques focus on creating new and exciting surfaces, as well as manipulating existing surfaces, and can be applied to everything from all-over fabrics to trims and edgings.

Readers will learn how to work with a variety of traditional and unconventional techniques, from couture beading to using a soldering iron to recreate stitches. This book is built upon the considerable lecturing experience of the two authors and is in effect a snapshot of some of the methods and principles that underpin the three-year degree course (BA Hons Textile Art and Artefact) in the National College of Art and Design, Dublin, Ireland that the authors have pioneered. It will inspire students as well as engaging with more experienced makers looking for new inspiration and techniques.

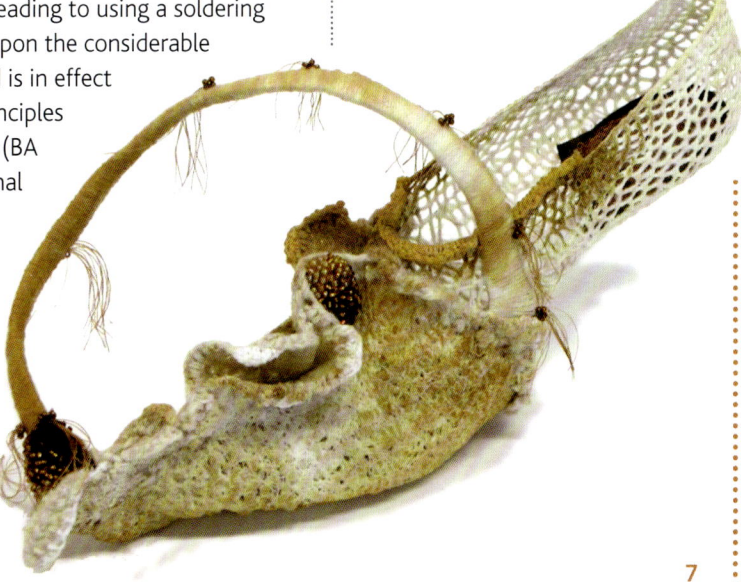

Helen McAllister, 'Heel-less shoe' form.
Photography by Tony Murphy.

Visual research

2

Our aim is to encourage you as readers to develop your skills in seeing, thinking, sampling and making decisions. These are the most important elements of being a designer. We also hope you will pick up some new textile skills and be inspired along the way to experiment and see the endless possibilities with these textile processes.

It is often hard to know just where to start. It can be overwhelming. Subject matter needs to have a depth, breadth and relevance that can be realistically accessed within whatever time frame you have on hand. Having selected a visual cornerstone to anchor a project, it is important to be individual, to try to find a unique design voice or visual handwriting.

We hope we can encourage you to avoid clichés and obvious interpretations. The first stage of that journey is in visual research, and we suggest that the more effort you put in at this stage, the more benefit you will get out in the long run. In this book we have narrowed down to a single source: the poppy. The poppy has become clichéd and is often used in a derivative and obvious way. If we look more closely we will see their drooping, pendant-like buds that burst from hairy vertical stems and after blooming become the brittle seed head. Poppies are rich in visual contrasts, from the frothy volume of the petals, their contrasting colours, their rich velvety stamens to the minute architectural precision of the seed heads.

This is a flower we have looked at during various periods of our careers, and in writing this book we have spent the last few years gathering research. Taking into account the fact that most species in the UK flower as early as March, most in late May to mid-July and some until September, it has meant that certain elements of the visual observation,

01 *Watercolour study of an opium poppy.*

documentation and research have only been possible in the summer. Responding to this natural rhythm and time frame is inevitable when collecting original visual research. Blooms can last anywhere from two days to two weeks, and many species are commonly found as garden weeds. There are many more unusual and varied species; however to see these requires more effort. We believe this is a visual source that has great appeal for many to enjoy. This book explores interpretations of the theme that range from 2D to 3D, and from representational to abstract. Our aim is for this to be a stimulating and informative aid that the more experienced practitioner can dip in and out of, whilst those new to these approaches can follow it stage by stage. There are also different methods of working with materials that can be applied to many other parallel sources or outcomes with a transferable approach.

We aim to demonstrate how just this one source, if we examine it in depth with integrity, intelligence, spontaneity and passion, can provide inspiration by virtue of its diverse range of colour, image, pattern, texture, surface, structure, proportion, composition, form and detail. The source may have potential for different approaches, so avoid the expected and look for more original directions. Poppies look so different at various stages of their life cycle. Inspiration may come from the veins and ridges of a dried-out seed head or a vibrant rippled petal.

We have developed a number of projects to exploit the range of outcomes that any one source can yield.

TEXTILE SURFACE MANIPULATION

02 *Common corn poppy* (Papaver rhoeas).

What is design?

Although this book uses the poppy as a theme to give continuity to a whole range of different products and styles, the design methods we will adopt can be applied to almost any theme or subject matter. Textile designers and makers work best when pursuing a set brief. This may be very detailed or more open-ended, but there are so many pathways we can follow, that some focus is essential. Your approach may be abstract, narrative or conceptual. Research methods can be applicable for all of these, as long as you know what you are trying to achieve. These projects focus on the realisation of research and sampling into functional objects. The same research and development processes apply to both textile designers and that of the craft/applied art practitioner, whether the designers work through print, weave, knit, embroidery or mixed media processes. The textile designer's work is sold through twice-yearly trade fairs in Europe and New York as part of the fashion cycle. For them it is often enough to leave the design at this stage as a paper or fabric sample, and sell it on to industry to achieve an end result. Textile designers work either in a freelance capacity for clients or as part of an agency or collective. In fashion fabrics they mostly work to seasonal trends and with very specific colour, image and design briefs. The designs are shown in groups of ten to twelve with a common colour palette, but with completely separate motifs or images. It is sometimes helpful to think of a group of designs as a family portrait.

VISUAL RESEARCH

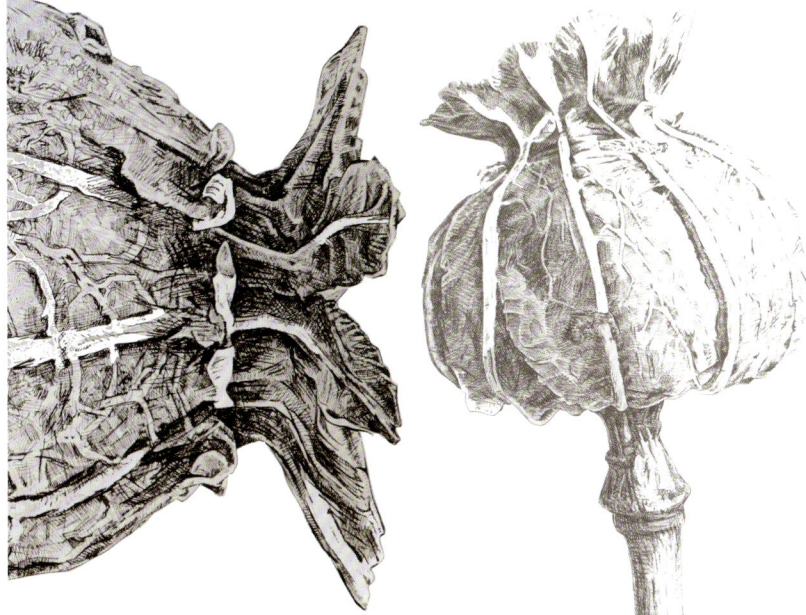

03

04

03 *Observed drawing of dried poppy seed heads.*

04 *Watercolour study of opium poppy and wasp.*

There is some kind of visual resemblance between the individual members (for example, a genetic trait like blond hair, big ears or a small nose), however it is important that there are no identical twins! If you sell one design from the group you must be sure that if your customer's competitors buy another design from the same collection they are not too similar.

The design process often begins with observational research, through looking at and recording as accurately as possible to become familiar with the subject matter. The approach and media used at this stage can be vital to inform the direction of the project. Some sense of final outcome will be vital, for example delicate or bold, abstract or representative, detailed or gestural.

Commercial textile designs are presented in three ways: as design ideas, *croquis* or in technical repeat. These are sold according to a fixed price range, regardless of how complicated the design may be. Textile design is one of the least copyright-protected professions within the design industry and there is an individual responsibility on ethical standards.

Design ideas can be as simple as a single piece of artwork or a page from a sketchbook, and are often bought as inspiration for other designers to develop.

TEXTILE SURFACE MANIPULATION

Croquis is the technical term for a design idea that looks as if it has been cut from a finished length of fabric. It has been developed to a point where there are sufficient complete design elements and an indication of repeat structure from which a repeat length can be manufactured. A technical repeat is where the design is completely resolved to specific technical requirement and ready for manufacture. Sometimes designs are engineered to fit a particular shape, garment or pattern piece. One such example is a scarf. Designer scarves should never look as though they have just been cut from a length of fabric, but the way they fall when worn should be considered. The classic square scarf nearly always has a border, and particular emphasis is placed on the corners.

Botanical research

With something as universal as flowers as a subject matter it is all too easy to pick visual elements at random; however with a little more effort you can use research to become informed and therefore more selective. It's not necessary to get sidetracked into becoming a botanist, but you can easily become a mini-expert on your subject. The flowers you use will be more realistic and correctly informed by this research. It is also an opportunity to make connections with people who already have a long-standing interest in this subject. Often these experts can be exceedingly generous, as they are only too happy to share their knowledge and passion.

05 *Initial CAD (computer-aided design) design idea, using fills and brushes in conjunction with a hand-drawn image.*

06 Croquis *design that indicates the essence of the repeat, without being completely technically resolved.*

07 *This square scarf idea is an example of a placement design, where the pattern is engineered to fit the shape of the product itself.*

VISUAL RESEARCH

08 *Papaver laciniatum, growing wild in a back garden.*

09 *Detailed scan showing how the sepals have broken away to reveal the soft petals of the corn poppy (Papaver rhoeas).*

There are over 700 species of poppies, ranging from herbaceous plants to shrubs and even small trees.

We can appreciate the different stages of growth from the 'lettuce' stage, where the plant builds up leaves before they grow into long slender stems with a mass of prickly leaves, to the forming of a bud, whose prickly sepals cup the delicate crumpled petals before opening to bloom. As the petals open they often have a concave shape that cups and protects the stamens that are the male reproductive part of the flower and the seed head or ovary that is the female reproductive part of the flower. As the smooth spherical capsule dries out, many tiny seeds are released through the pores under the compound pistil with its ridges, radiating from a central point. All these elements of the plants have a variety of different shapes, textures and forms to inspire us. We will document these stages of growth and look at inspiration from vibrant plants through to withered petals and dried leaves.

10 *Image of scattered opium poppy petals.*

11 *Opium poppy, side view close-up detail of the ovary, showing the gaps under the pistils where the seeds escape.*

12 *Detailed scan of three dried poppy leaves, showing their bristles.*

TEXTILE SURFACE MANIPULATION

Different wild species have developed in different parts of the globe. The North American Californian poppies are part of the *Eschscholzia* family, ranging from bright yellow and orange to red. They are best known for the way the blooms unfurl their four petals to follow the sun and close in dull weather. The cupped paper-thin petals shelter a whorl of many stamens. The plants are perennials and their fern-like blue-green foliage forms a mound of low-lying shrubs. Their cousins, *Platystemon californicus*, are commonly known rather whimsically as cream cups, while the California wild poppy, *Papaver heterophyllum*, revels in the contrast of shaded petals (with yellow tips and red centres) as a dramatic backdrop to its bright yellow anthers.

13 *The elegant leaf and furled petals of a pink California poppy.*

14 *Mexican* matilija *tree poppy.*

15 Eschscholzia, *California poppies. Initial research board looking at shape, texture and colour.*

16 *Initial sketchbook page showing colour and texture ideas.*

VISUAL RESEARCH

In north-west Mexico the tree poppy has many variants, most notably *Dendromecon*, which also has satiny yellow petals, and *Romneya coulteri* or Mexican *Matilija* tree poppy with its crinkly white petals and vibrant yellow centres of smaller, tightly curled petals. *Argemone mexicana* is also known as the devil's fig, due to its resemblance to the fruit but with venomous prickles. In a peculiar and incongruous misnomer it is also known as the golden thistle of Peru. In the Mediterranean we find *Papaver pilosum* with the capsule-shaped fruit that is its key distinguishing element.

Throughout the Himalayas and western China there is also the dramatic *Meconopsis* family. The name stems from the Greek word *opsis* ('resemblance'). In European gardens the Nepal blue or *Meconopsis betonicifolia* with its four almost translucent, bright blue petals caused a horticultural sensation in 1924 with its introduction to Kew Gardens, London by F. Kingdon Ward. Its only European cousin is *Meconopsis cambrica* or Welsh poppy, a tufted plant with delicate yellow petals that is a native of shady places amongst rocky landscapes.

The Oriental poppy *Papaver orientale* is native to the Middle East and has extra large decorative petals in a deep scarlet that contrast with its velvety mass of inky purple-black stamens. We do not need to see perfect specimens, sometimes the weather-ravaged blooms may be more visually exciting.

17 *Raindrops on Nepal blue or* Meconopsis betonicifolia *in Benvarden Gardens, Co. Antrim, Northern Ireland.*

18 *Mood board inspired by* Meconopsis.

19 *The luscious scarlet of the oriental poppy provides initial inspiration for pattern and colour.*

TEXTILE SURFACE MANIPULATION

20

The opium poppy *Papaver somniferum* has associations with its narcotic derivatives (morphine, heroin and codeine) and their use throughout history. This sap is housed within the ovary and is harvested as a latex before the seed head dries out. In cultivation, these have many beautiful sub-species that have been bred to create a wide variety of colours and petals. We have looked at one of the most common garden poppy or breadseed poppies, the Hungarian blue, with its four deeply ridged petals in a pale blue, lavender and almost lilac colour. The characteristic black 'thumbprints' on each petal form a visual cross shape that acts as a foil for the white stamens with long filaments and bead-like anthers that contain the pollen. These surround the acid lime-green capsule with its compound pistil with thirteen ridges. The blue-green seed pods are often used in flower displays.

Prince of Orange is a perennial double oriental poppy with six petals of a vivid scarlet orange that contrast with deep purple centres. The stalks and sepals, which are the two leaf-like outermost whorls of the flower in the bud stage, have a multitude of tiny bristles or hairs.

Papaver laciniatum also has a mass of skinny forked petals and comes in varieties in tones of deep crimson through to purple, which resemble a ruffled pompom.

The most opulent and dramatic peony poppies *Papaver paeoniflorium* have double compacted blooms and range from scarlet, violet and purple through to palest pink.

20 *Observational drawing in ink of a fading bloom of* Papaver orientalis.

21 *Coral Reef, pale salmon-coloured oriental poppy. Photograph courtesy of Claire Conway.*

22 *Weather-ravaged poppy.*

23 Papaver somniferum, *opium poppy*.

24 The exuberant stamens contrast against the dark centres of the crinkled petals of Papaver somniferum, *Hungarian blue*.

25 Detail of stamens of the opium poppy.

26 Side profile of Hungarian blue in bloom.

27 Top left *Head of seed pod showing compound pistils*. Top right *Cross-section of ovary showing structure of seed chambers*. Bottom *Side view of ovary*.

28 Papaver laciniatum, *or pompom poppy*.

29 Peony poppy the 'double black' Papaver paeoniflorium.

30 The purple velvety stamens of Prince of Orange, a flamboyant scarlet Papaver orientalis.

TEXTILE SURFACE MANIPULATION

Interpretation

It is important to consider how your subject matter may have other subtexts or meanings that a viewer may elicit from them. Textile artists deliberately use these associations to engage in a dialogue with their audience. For designers a less confrontational approach may be desirable where visual appreciation is the main consideration. Poppies have symbolised sleep, dreams, death and resurrection. In Persia they symbolised true love.

Perhaps the best-known poppy is the frequently depicted and often stylised corn poppy *Papaver rhoeas* with its trademark four round scarlet petals. In fact it is such a vibrant symbol that anything scarlet red is often referenced to poppies. We see many representations of summer cornfields with their scattering of red poppies. Van Gogh painted seven paintings of *Rhoeas* poppies and his 'Field with Poppies' (1890) is depicted in endless art history textbooks.

The corn poppies that are prevalent in the fields of France and Belgium have become synonymous with depictions of World War I. This is mainly due to the last lines of the famous poem 'In Flanders Field', by Lieutenant Colonel John McCrae. It was written in 1915 in Ypres, Belgium, where McCrae was a doctor commanding a dressing station.

31 *Common corn poppy, showing the petals separated from the stamens and seed head.*

32 *Close-up detail of Poppy Appeal wreath, showing paper leaves and moulded plastic centres.*

VISUAL RESEARCH

In the UK the Royal British Legion uses the corn poppy as its iconic symbol. With two pressed paper leaves and plastic stem for a lapel badge, it is widely worn on Armistice Day. The stylised image of two red petals and a black centre has been a symbol of remembrance throughout the Commonwealth since World War I. They are made in a factory in England and are part of the annual Poppy Appeal, which raised about £35 million in 2011. As an alternative initiative to help war veterans Lady Haig's Poppy Factory was established in Scotland and produces about five million handmade, distinctive four-petal poppies that are also worn as plastic and pleated-paper badges or as a printed image on stickers. All of these are sold to raise funds for the armed forces, their families and veterans. The poppies are also made into commemorative wreaths and it is hard to see a circular composition of poppies without associating it with those that are displayed on war memorials on Remembrance Sunday.

Image 34 shows an idea that was inspired by a family photograph of Corporal William Holman and the war memorials in the town square and Little Bowden Church, Market Harborough, Leicestershire.

When creating anything that relies on such deeply symbolic imagery, it is important that you take a moment to be sure of your intentions. Mentally take a step back to consider whether your design could be misinterpreted by anyone.

33 *Design idea inspired by Nigel Cheney's great grandfather, Corporal William Holman, who died at Vimy Ridge, Arras, in WWI.*

34 *Alternative design idea inspired by Nigel Cheney's family photographic archive of Corporal William Holman. The signatures come from a postcard kept by his grandson during national service in the 1950s.*

TEXTILE SURFACE MANIPULATION

Becoming inspired

The sideways leaps of connections and influences can often bring about the most exciting results. Juxtaposition, dislocation and the unexpected change of scale are all post-modern tools that contemporary designers employ with dramatic effect. Serendipity can play an important part, but it is unlikely to find you if you hide at home under the duvet. It is important to get out and about, either by doing something as dramatic as foreign travel or as mundane as visiting a local junk shop or car boot sale.

35 and 36 *Objects on display in the private collection of Helen McAllister.*

VISUAL RESEARCH

Seeing (observing and recording)

When you have identified your source, it is important to spend time looking, observing and finding ways to record this information. The actual handling of the source makes for greater learning and understanding. Physically holding an object gives us another level of understanding that synthesises touch with imagery. How you capture this is vital in terms of what methods you use to record the visual information. It's a little like the classic 'chicken or egg' question, but you have to start somewhere! Outcome and approach are so interdependent for helpful translation from source to technique. For example, if you know you want to produce something lace-like as a final outcome, this should inform your entire approach to what you look at and the way you document it. In contrast, if you are driven by the source itself, this should suggest the materials, scale and qualities you aim to translate through textile thinking and processes. Of course there are clichés to avoid in very obvious sources with direct translations; replication denies the creative process of interpretation and morphing. Try to establish a different angle from which to look at your research.

37 *Experimental drawings of bud and seed head that have been manipulated using CAD.*

TEXTILE SURFACE MANIPULATION

When working with textiles we suggest a hands-on approach at all times. There is no exact work structure or single method to follow. As you become more experienced you will develop a number of tried and tested approaches. We would encourage everyone to be flexible and not be prescriptive. There is never one linear route or blueprint to follow: that would be too easy! However you work, it is important that you are able to look closely at your source. We do suggest that some system of working across various formats will allow for this flexibility. Whether it is a number of initial ideas pages, an inspirational mood board or research worksheets, it is vital to have some way of physically combining the visual elements of image, surface, texture, shape, image, pattern and colour.

Colour is the most essential part of a textile designer's repertoire. We have an empathy, understanding and sensitivity to colour that is often intuitive and responds to the zeitgeist or underground trends that textile students are often sensitive to. What is imperative is that we see colour and materiality as interdependent. The same colour tint has a totally different sense depending on the material it is applied to. We believe there is no such thing as an ugly colour, merely a colour in the wrong place, or perhaps in the wrong material. Colour is inseparable from material, so it is important that when we think about colour in textiles it is in association with material finish, surface and texture. From matt, iridescent, neon or lustre to high-shine and patent finishes, threads and fabrics come in such a dazzling array of alternatives that they provide endless possibilities. In deciding on a colour palette we need to think in terms of materials rather than just coloured paints or pencils.

Research with a camera

Photography is an essential tool for the modern designer. Digital cameras have become so sophisticated that with very little technical knowledge many things are possible: now everyone can take a good photograph. It can be all too seductive to think that this is the beginning and end of research. Photography can provide much information, but there is a dislocation between a pixellated image on screen and the physical activity of responding to this with media.

In scanning poppies we noticed that both the pollen from the blooms and the seeds from the dried husks of the ovaries left the scanner plate covered in small dots. We have used this polka-dot pattern as a stylistic element across many of the projects. In some it is the pointillist nature of beading, while in others it is an added digital layer in the print designs.

38

38 *Withered petals surrounding the elongated stamens and seed head of a California poppy. We see the poppy seeds surrounding the image.*

Research by drawing

One of the hardest things for us to accept is that there is no right or wrong way to draw. From an early age, certain perceptions of what makes a good drawing prevail. As textile designers we can explore many different ways of rendering marks, textures and surfaces. It is important to remember it's not about making pictures. The challenges of working with different media and grounds will give surprising results. In textile research we enjoy breaking the rules and combining, layering or contrasting different media and techniques. In conventional painting we see a value in making a single medium reflect or capture a number of different properties. Skilled artists can make any individual medium represent contrasts such as transparency and opacity. In textiles we would suggest you actively attempt to find materials to help you do this. Collage is a successful technique in contrasting properties, for instance tracing paper and brown paper might capture qualities with far less effort and more effect. Experimental mark-making and collage inform and infuse works that develop using multiple materials. From instantaneous approaches such as a rubbing of tree bark, marbling, or puncturing holes in paper to a detailed, sustained, academic drawing over many hours, all paperwork can be useful.

If working on location it may not be possible to work with some media that are too messy, or to be able to spend a long time there. Try to collect enough information to be able to reconstruct the key elements when you are back in your studio or workshop. Decide what information you want your drawing to record. List these elements and try tackling them separately with the knowledge that textile sampling will pull the elements back together. For example, if you are looking at a clump of poppies in a garden, decide what it is that interests you. You might enjoy the composition, the colour combinations, the shapes of the individual poppies and the contrasts in texture. Rather than spending a long time trying to capture this in a detailed painting in one medium, tackle the elements separately and in the most efficient manner. You could use photography to record all of the elements, moving around and stepping close with a macro lens then moving back to capture the whole scene. These images will not necessarily give you everything, but will act as a reminder and will complement the other information.

Adjectives are our friends and provide something to measure your textile work against. As a project develops we can sometimes lose sight of the driving force. If your overriding aim is to make something delicate, then that is a great word to pin up and use to interrogate

39 Colour board inspired by foliage and petals of a Coral Reef oriental poppy. The stripes are created in the CAD software by selecting a single row of the image and using this as a fill.

your work. Does the description match what you have actually made? If we described a source as 'crinkled' or 'chalky', then these words are good to test material selection against. You might start a worksheet and do some gestural drawings to capture the shapes, or explore colour possibilities.

Collecting materials

Throughout this book we will look at how the selection of materials is intrinsic to the success of each project. We will encourage you to consider not just the fine fabrics, beads and threads that are associated with traditional embroidery, but also to ask yourself what can be a material and how you can change or alter it to capture the qualities in your research and relate to the purpose of your project.

Most textile designers and makers are magpies. Only by collecting different elements that appeal to you will you build a storehouse of materials to work from. The design process itself is often quite organic, allowing ideas to grow and change. Being inspired by materials and their properties matters more than just going out with a shopping list of goodies to buy. We are great believers in serendipity, and would encourage you to think laterally. For example if your research looks at a broken surface, consider what you can find that has an open structure. This could be in the form of holes or perforations (can you make these yourself?) or a grid-like structure such as an open weave, metal lattice or mesh.

Social responsibility in design

As designers it is important that you think about the end user. Identifying exactly who your work would appeal to is one way to begin. If you know your market well and can fulfill that customer's desires, you will find the work you make far more rewarding in every sense of the word. The handmade is an important element in this book and even when these projects embrace machine or even digital processes, there is always something individual in how these are used to create an object, garment or accessory. It may be upcycling, adding to something that has already been made, or it may be deconstructing something to take it back to its raw materials to reuse them. Whether it is through designing for a commission, as a present for a loved one or as a small business venture, making objects with a specific person, muse or customer in mind is the key to creating something that will be cherished.

Upcycling

Upcycling is a trendy new word that has replaced the term 'recycling'; it is when the reconstituted version is better than the original! But this isn't new to embroiderers, who have always done this from frugality or thriftiness, and have always known how to see the potential in materials and objects other people have finished with, to turn every scrap of material into a jewel, and to transform something discarded into something amazing. You may be making modern heirlooms or a luxury gift, but by considering just who would enjoy what you make, their taste in colour, feel and usability, you will ensure a successful outcome. We believe that it is possible to create something individual and special whose lifespan will far exceed anything you can buy on the high street.

40 *Cotton threads in a wide range of colours.*

Repeat structures

3

It is extremely useful for a surface pattern designer to understand the basics of repeat design, particularly if an item is going to be produced commercially. After many years of being unfashionable, these have recently seen a return in fashion and interiors. A good starting point is repeats that are formed from block motif shapes. Often the aim of a repeat is to make the repeat itself as invisible as possible, where all the spaces around individual motifs are evenly and harmoniously distributed.

All-over distributions are created using the principles of a number of multiple motifs, units or elements that are mathematically placed using grids to ensure a perfect technical repeat.

Motif

All repeats are centred around an individual motif or element and the space between this and its next appearance in the repeat.

Full drop

The most basic repeat, where each element is tiled next to each other left to right along a horizontal row and vertical columns, all evenly spaced.

Fractional drops

This is where the unit is offset at a fraction of the unit, rather than a whole unit. The most common are half- and third-drops.

REPEAT STRUCTURES

41 Left *A motif comprising four petals.*
Top right *A full-drop repeat, where the motifs are at the same horizontal and vertical distance.* Bottom right *A half-drop repeat, where the motifs are the same horizontal distance apart, while vertically each motif drops half the length of its neighbour.*

42 *Two variations of the same motif distributed in a half-drop structure where the spacing is different*

43 Left *Third-drop motif made up of nine elements.* Right *Repeat; the black grid boxes indicate the repeat motif dropped a third in each column. For a more even repeat we could move the columns closer together.*

Half-drop

The designs are seen as columns that are each offset by half the length of the repeat drop.

Brick repeat

A half-drop turned through 90°. The motif repeats along the horizontal axis, however each row is offset by half the width of the repeat unit. This resembles the structure of a brick wall.

Third drop

The designs are seen as columns that are each offset by a third of the length of the repeat drop. It takes three columns before the repeat is complete on the horizontal as well as the vertical. Again, this creates a strong visual diagonal in the finished repeat.

TEXTILE SURFACE MANIPULATION

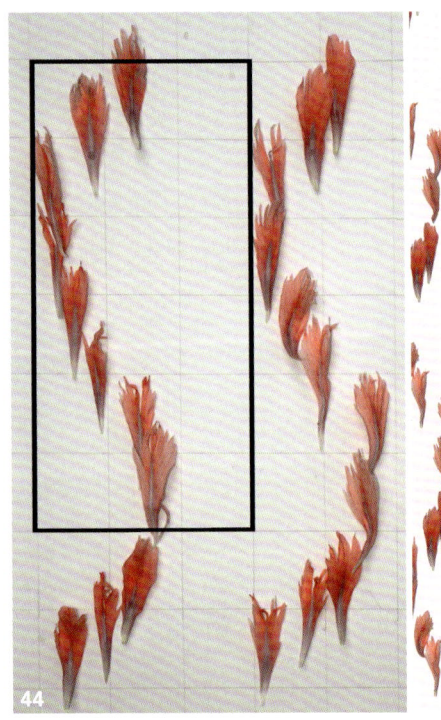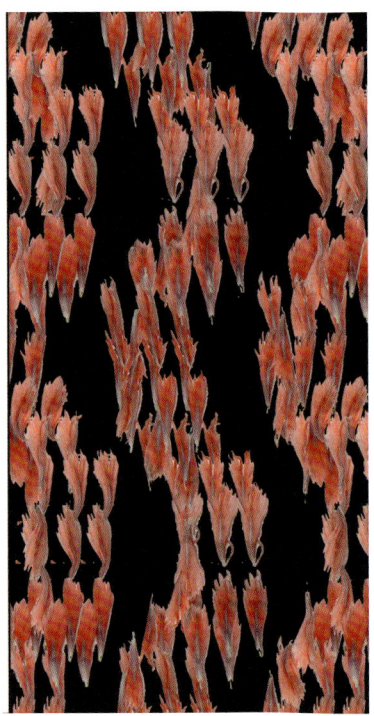

44 Left *A serpentine structure using petals from a* Laciniatum *poppy. The grid structure underneath ensures a successful layout.* Middle *The structure repeated with even spacing.* Right *Uneven spacing and alternative ground colour gives a different feeling to the repeat.*

Serpentine

Smooth, repetitive, oscillating, undulating or wavy (sinusoidal) lines that resemble reptilian movement. Each line is normally symmetrical. The patterns nest into each other with a full-drop repeat. The proportions can be altered for thick or thin waves.

Ogee

A curve shaped like the letter 'S' that comprises two arcs that curve in opposite senses.

We can create a similar effect with a serpentine that is mirrored on the vertical to create the 'ogee' shape.

Border

Any design that is weighted to a particular edge. The pattern may or may not repeat in one direction only. Often this is used at a hem or edge of a garment.

45 Left *By angling four leaves within a grid we create the basic unit for an ogee repeat.* Right *The ogee unit is repeated with a basic block structure. In this example each unit is mirrored to create a half-drop effect. The repeat is characterised by the negative diamond shapes formed in the centre of each unit.*

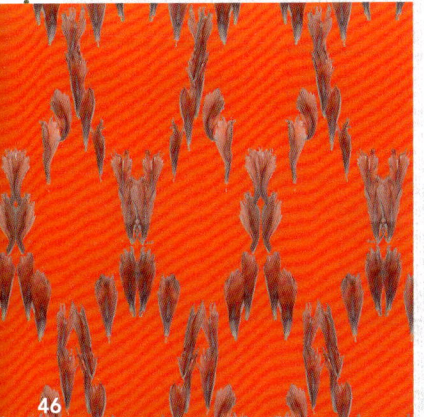

46 *By mirroring each column in the serpentine we create a faux ogee repeat.*

47 Left *Repeat motif of oriental poppy silhouette in serpentine layout.* Right *Same motif in ogee structure.*

48 *Border repeat of photographic motifs.*

TEXTILE SURFACE MANIPULATION

Spot repeats

To achieve an even distribution, floating individual elements need to follow a regular pattern. The elements can be larger than the grid square, which will ensure they overlap. It can help to think of the spot grids as following the principle of a sudoku puzzle. The challenge is balancing the placement of all the elements within a grid to achieve harmony. In spot structures only one element can be in each row and column.

5-spot

Working within a 5 x 5 grid, follow the formula (where the rows left to right are A, B, C etc. and the columns from top to bottom are 1, 2, 3 etc.). For the 5-spot it is A5, B3, C1, D4, E2.

Grounds surrounding 5-spot

You can develop an alternative to the simple spot structures by leaving some squares empty and filling the space around them with elements.

6-spot

Using the same principle, this is worked on a 6 x 6 grid: A6, B4, C2, D5, E1, F3.

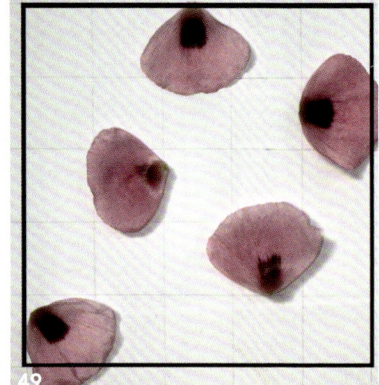 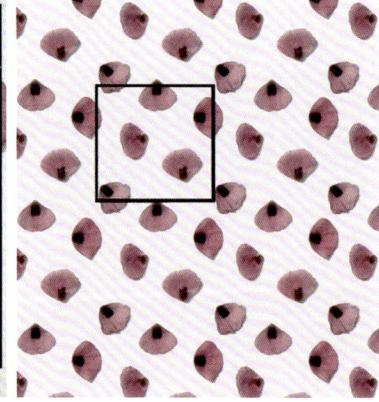

49 Left *5-spot layout over a 5 x 5 grid.* Right *The block in repeat.*

 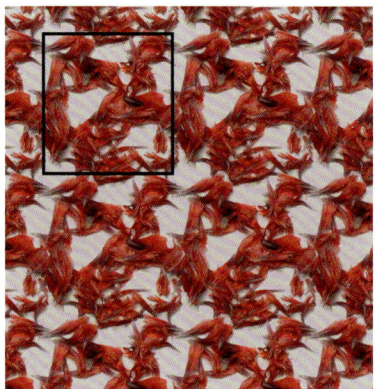

50 Left *The petals are placed to leave the 5-spot repeat empty.* Right *The unit in repeat.*

 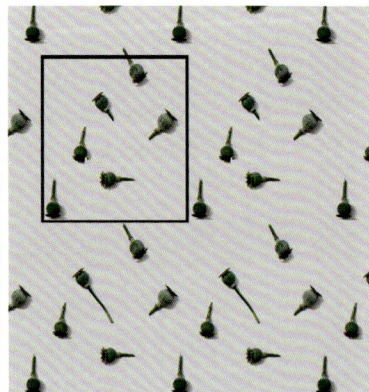

51 Left *The 6-spot unit over a 6 x 6 grid.* Right *The unit in repeat.*

REPEAT STRUCTURES

7-spot

Using the same principle, this is worked on a 7 x 7 grid: A7, B5, C3, D1, E6, F3, G2.

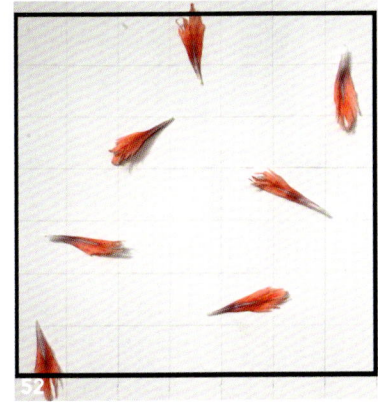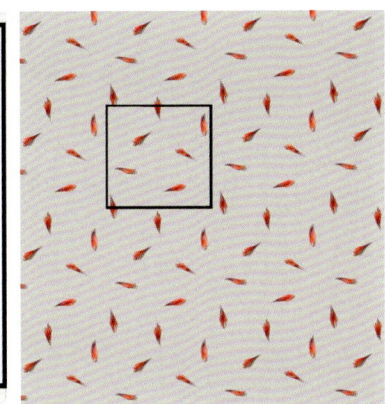

52 Left *The 7-spot unit over a 7 x 7 grid.* Right *The unit in repeat.*

Chevron

An inverted 'v' or zigzag pattern where the elements are set at an angle and mirrored before being set in a full-drop repeat. The fine spiky petals of the peony poppies create a shard-like shape that can easily form chevrons. By varying how close together we place the chevron lines, we achieve very different structures.

53 Left *Chevron unit over a 4 x 2 grid.* Middle *The unit in repeat.* Right *Alternative scale and ground colour.*

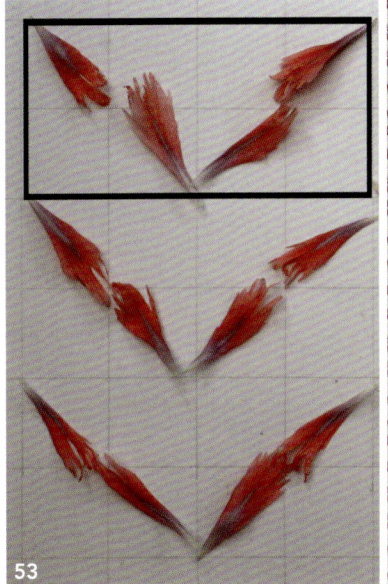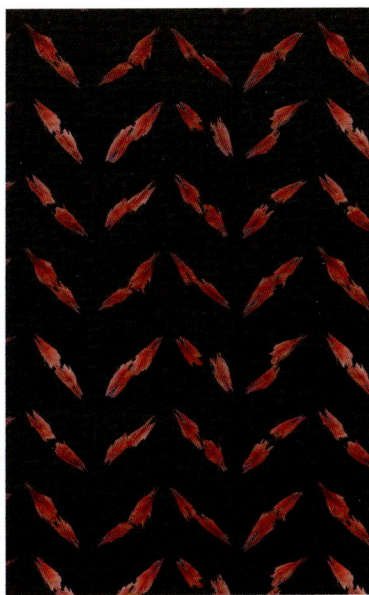

31

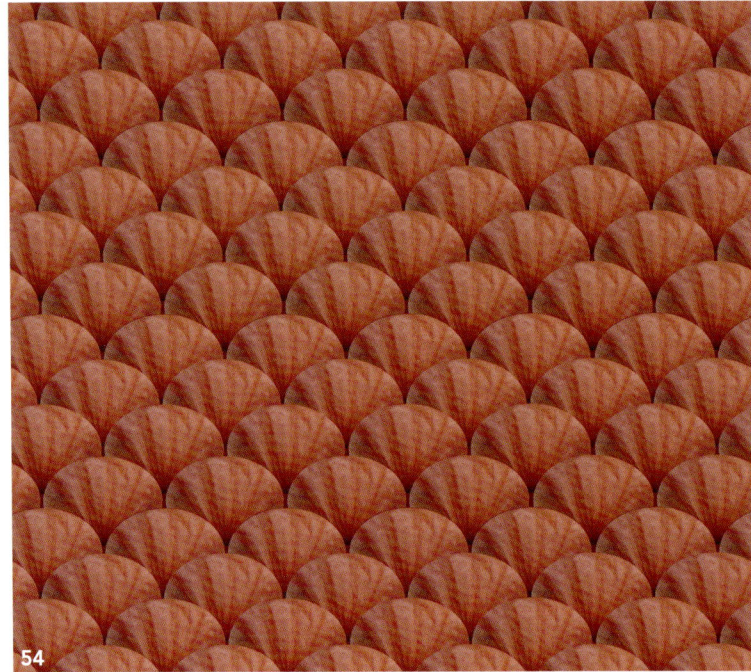

54 *A single oriental poppy petal, cropped into the clamshell shape and repeated.*

Clamshell

A typical repeat pattern in patchwork, this uses overlapping arcs to create rows of interlocking circular forms. The poppy petal itself makes a natural clamshell shape, so the repeat is simple to manipulate to relate to these shapes.

Other ways to explore repeats

The diagrams so far show standard repeats where all the elements are of equal size. To create more dramatic effects:
- explore different scale elements within a unit to achieve different results with the same structure
- mirror some of the elements within a repeat to provide alternative rhythms
- remember that each element has a direction as well as its position within the structure, which can be rotated to change rhythm
- explore more sensuous and linear repeats where the individual elements have a more fluid shape and are often intertwined.

We can follow the build-up of a complex repeat one element at a time, over a 6 x 6 grid, each in a different 6-spot repeat layout. As the motifs are bigger than the grid square, this ensures a complicated overlap. It is important that each element is placed in the same order from left to right row by row, and top to bottom, column by column.

Building surfaces: constructing or creating a fabric from scratch

4

Working with soluble fabrics

Working from a single yarn we can consider various ways to construct a fabric. Knit, weave, interlacing and lace are all techniques that interconnect a continuous length of yarn to create a structure. The sewing machine provides a much quicker way to create these materials. Embroiderers often use a variety of techniques. Working free machine embroidery over a soluble base material is something many textile practitioners fall in love with. It can be a magical transformation to see the structure that you have stitched away on for hours change with the addition of a little water: the ground dissolves and leaves the tracery of stitch work.

As an embroidered type of lace-making, it can capture all the qualities of delicacy, elegance and intricacy.

Sampling is always best approached with the question 'What happens if...?'. This project extends that basic technique by using loose, open knitted structures as an existing structure that forms the basis for chunkier or more dynamic surfaces.

When creating a fabric from scratch it is important that the threads interlace to create a robust structure. Here is a technique where the stitch can be used as both structure and decoration.

55 *A lace fabric created using a soluble fabric and machine embroidery of a poppy motif over a hand-knitted ground.*

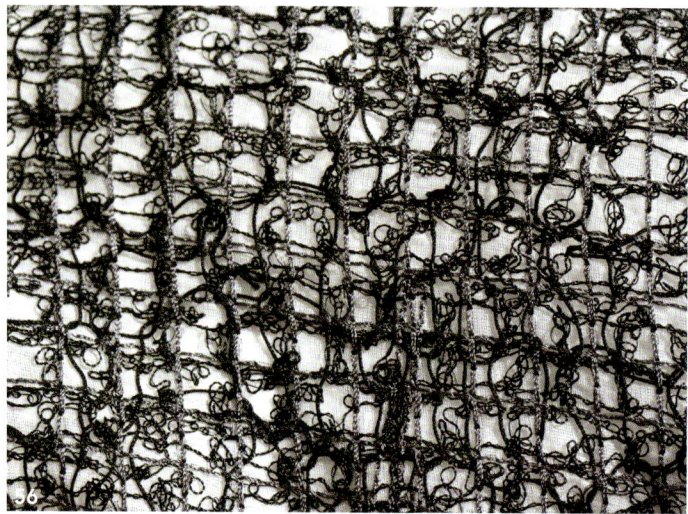

Knitted structures

Begin by creating a ground fabric of a very loosely knitted material. You can do this by either knitting the holey fabric yourself or unravelling an existing knit. This could be as fine as laddering tights or as bold as dropping stitches in an Aran jumper. For those who can knit, this is a way of generating a unique structure. With the change of tension, different effects will result, and even dropped stitches will add interest. It is not necessarily about producing perfect even structures, as the embroidery will stabilise the final fabric and change the knitted structure and surface.

Some things to try when knitting a ground structure:
- experiment with oversized or alternative needles (wooden dowels, etc.); many craft fairs sell really exciting large needles
- try different yarns, from fluffy mohair to matt crochet cotton or even a shiny viscose yarn; combinations of similar or contrasting yarns can produce spectacular effects
- work with a dip-dyed yarn: many are available commercially or you can explore dyeing yourself.

Some things to try in manipulating an existing knit:
- start with a knitted dishcloth and snip in several places
- start with an old pair of tights and ladder them
- start with a chunky jumper and let some of the stitches drop, or even chop into small sections and scatter between layers of soluble base fabric.

56 *Soluble fabric showing the creation of an interlacing grid structure of machine embroidery.*

57 *Colour board.*

BUILDING SURFACES: CONSTRUCTING OR CREATING A FABRIC FROM SCRATCH

  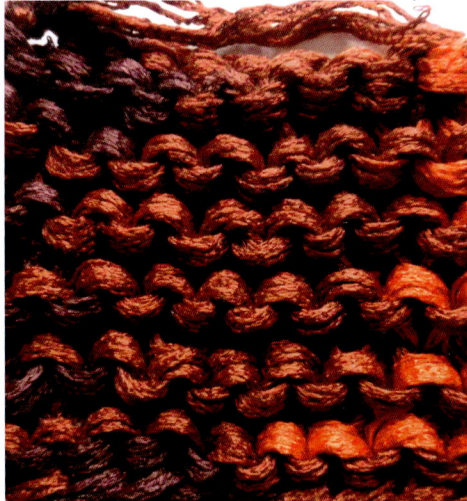

58 Left and centre *Open knit structures using oversized needles with finer yarns.* Right *Dip-dyed yarn used to create a dense garter-stitch structure.*

Creating the knitted base fabric

The bigger the needle and the finer the yarn, the more lacy the knit structure will be.

You may want to work with lace stitches or drop stitches; stocking stitch (knit a row, purl a row), or garter stitch (knit every row) ribs will make the final fabric more stretchy. Fancy yarns may be spun with extra texture or slubs in them that will add to the final texture.

Stitched textures

The diverse structures in the test samples are all inspired by the dried and broken husk of the poppy head (see image 27). These lace-like patterns are built in several layers. An initial grid can be built using a domestic sewing machine with a straight foot, sewing backwards and forwards in both horizontally and vertically to create a grid (see image 59). Use the machine foot as a guide to ensure even distance between stitch lines.

You can decide to only have lines in one direction, work only on a diagonal or with a much wider grid. All of these variations will give a different handle to the final fabric, so consider its purpose. If you want it to drape, use lines further apart. Working on the diagonal or bias will distort the fabric and make it fall elegantly. Working a dense, close grid will make fabric more robust and rigid.

TEXTILE SURFACE MANIPULATION

Selecting which type of soluble fabric works best for you

Cold-water-soluble fabrics come in many different types and are available from craft shops and various suppliers on the Internet. The most common forms are a plastic-like film, one brand is SOLVY that works well for hand stitch; this is rather like a shower curtain (we find it quite difficult to use), or a non-woven, more papery type. We tend to use Madeira CWSF, as it is tough and comes in 1m-wide rolls of up to 50m.

Making the 'sandwich'

Use the soluble fabric as a bottom layer to build onto. It can be helpful to draw a grid or pattern piece onto this layer with pencil. It gives you an outline to make sure you keep the flimsy or deconstructed knitted fabric as even as possible. Carefully place the knitted fabric on top, making sure the tension is spread out evenly and there are no folds or lumps. As this is a 'cut and sew' technique, it doesn't matter if the knit layer extends beyond the grid shape as you will be cutting away any excess.

Finally, cover with another layer of the soluble fabric to create a sandwich, with the soluble fabric on the outside.

Stitching

Always use an embroidery hoop to hold the various layers together while you are working.

Try to work in a grid format or with overlapping circular motions.

You can work from both sides, swapping back and forth, playing with tension effects and colour-blending by selecting different-coloured top and bobbin threads.

59 *The grid of machine stitch embeds the chunky knit and stabilises its stretchy structure.*

60 *Embroidered grid extends beyond knit to create the start of a lace border.*

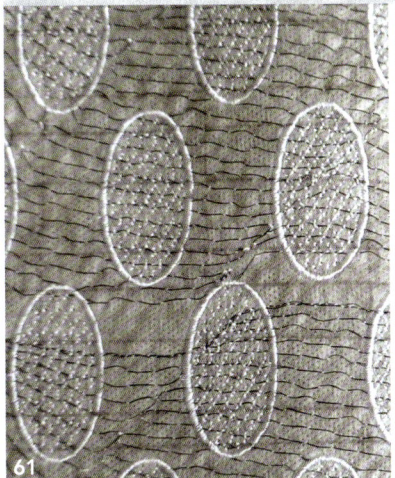

61 Left *Unwashed*. Centre *Washed*. Right *Spot worked in alternative colour on more open ground*.

62 *This sample shows how the rhythmic pattern of the embroidery has no interconnecting structure, so when washed the threads just flop.*

63 Left *Unwashed*. Right *Washed*.

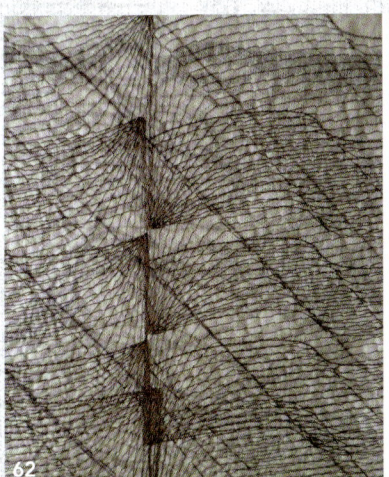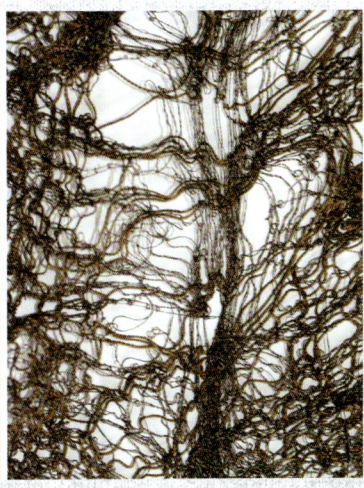

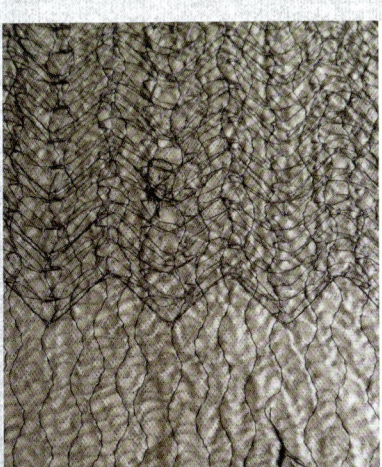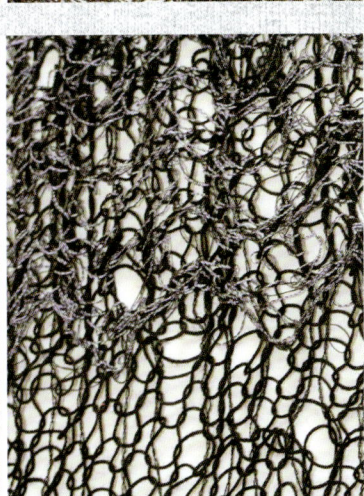

TEXTILE SURFACE MANIPULATION

64 Left *Parallel lines of set pattern of spot stitches are worked over a knit structure to create a bobbly fabric.* Right *Detail showing how spots are formed with radiating stitches.*

Adding texture

Over these basic knitted structures more decorative or high-relief embellished patterns can be added. These can be solid motifs, linear rhythms or satin-stitch shapes. The petals and leaves themselves have given ideas for the repeat patterns.

The samples

When you have finished sewing, tear off any excess soluble fabric from the edges. To dissolve the fabric, make sure you check the manufacturer's instructions, as all types have slightly different properties.

Normally you can just hold the sample under a cold tap, or leave it to soak in a bucket. Rinsing is important: in very concentrated areas of stitching, you may need to gently rub the stitches with something like a pastry brush.

Be careful that any dye doesn't run. This is particularly important if you are working with strong colour contrasts, or hand-dyed yarns. You will soon see by trial and error that machine lines that don't connect will just fall apart.

Pitfalls

Even for the most careful and experienced users, sometimes the stitched textile comes out of the wash as an unattractive lump! This is particularly true with small fragments. If the work is particularly delicate it can be

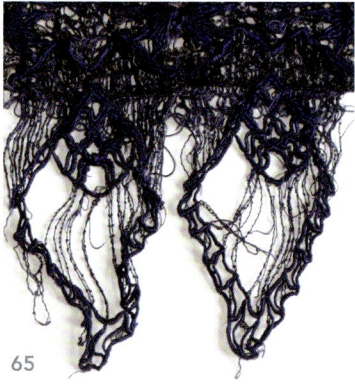

65 Top *Unwashed sample showing geometric border.* Bottom *Washed border showing how the long radiating lines need more cross lines to establish a robust structure.*

BUILDING SURFACES: CONSTRUCTING OR CREATING A FABRIC FROM SCRATCH

useful to tack the work in progress to a temporary base fabric. This will keep the fabric under tension and will be easy to reshape after washing.

Obviously it is important test your materials for colour-fastness and shrinkage. Often the starches that form the soluble material are not completely dissolved and the final fabric is hard or doesn't have the lovely handle that the threads or knit should have. This is easily remedied by further washing. We recommend you also wash the textile with a fabric softener. You can allow the fabric to dry naturally or press it into shape with a dry iron. Be careful with iron temperatures: remember the nature of the fibres and don't destroy these with overheating.

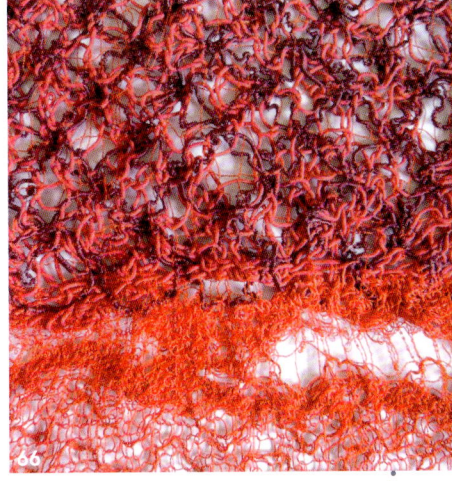

66 The pattern is disrupted and broken to expose areas of the knit with pulled or dropped stitches.

67 Sample showing how a stitched structure of overlapping circles, worked over a bought stretch fabric (shocking pink leggings) creates a gathered and manipulated surface.

68 Poppy motif worked over a surface of embroidered spots on a found knit.

69 Detail showing the formation of the stitches that create the machine-set patterns that form the ground embroidery.

70 Poppy motif over open knit ground.

71 Stylised petal motif over open knit ground.

Project 1. Felted scarf

We have realised this technique into a simple scarf. It is felted, which means it is knitted in quite an open structure and then deliberately shrunk to make a dense material and is designed to be a short 'cravat'-style accessory.

For a finished 15cm x 1.5m scarf in a wool/mohair mix double-knit weight, you will need to knit a ground which is about 25cm x 3m. Using 12mm (US size 17) needles, cast on 25 stitches and work approx 300 rows of garter stitch (knit every row) or until scarf measures 3m.

This fabric is the base for the scarf. As you can feel in its initial state it is quite stretchy and floppy and catches quite easily.

Sandwich this between two layers of cold-water-soluble film. You will need to tack this to the bottom layer to keep the edges straight.

For this scarf we want the fibres to felt, therefore you will need to wash it in the washing machine on a 40° delicate cycle. Remember you can never unfelt, so shrink gradually! Using some fabric softener is essential.

From the initial sampling and the development of this project we can see countless alternatives. By experimenting with the base fabric, stitch pattern and decorative motifs. By changing the shape and proportion of the scarf, ultimately this ratio will define a successful and contemporary product. Scarves are always in fashion, but the weight and dimensions change for both men and women each season.

How they are worn – knotted, draped or tied – is also essential. With this technique it is simple to develop the product into an alternative outcome: a snood. This is a long, skinny scarf that is joined, or knitted on circular needles to create a loop with no ends. The seam that makes the loop can be constructed before washing so that the product comes out completely finished. We can also twist the fabric before joining the raw edges. This will give more movement to the snood.

72 Left *Knitted base fabric before embroidery.* Right *Detail of embroidered and felted fabric.*

73 *Cravat-style short felted scarf detail. Photography by Philip White. Model: Polina Yakobson.*

74 *Detail of embroidered and felted scarf.*

TEXTILE SURFACE MANIPULATION

Detached buttonhole stitch

Indeed there are endless stitches and techniques one could learn, yet a lot of stitches are variations of key base stitches. As tutors of contemporary embroidery, we believe in taking ownership of a stitch or technique and making it your own. Every embroiderer seems to have a favourite stitch, one that they use, exploit, and show in many manifestations. Much has been written and researched about what is a very intimate dialogue and relationship between the endless repetition of stitching and the maker. This author came to this realisation fairly late in life, having been hooked on embroidery from the age of 16. Where youth lacked the patience for handwork and the discipline for hand techniques, ironically now with the arrival of patience and discipline, the eyesight and the stiffening of hands are starting to impede. The domestic machine, large-scale, two-dimensional works has now been replaced by small scale, three-dimensionally hand embroidered. Out of this came a love for a stitch, 'my' stitch, that of buttonholing. As educators we see the importance of not just knowing a stitch but exploiting it to see how far you can take it, how different it can look by use of changes in scale and in what you sew with.

Buttonhole stitch is also known as blanket stitch; both names imply a particular function or use. Yet this stitch is actually endless in how it can look, it is so simple: the needle goes through a loop of thread and that is all! It can be used as an edging, it can be used to create a surface that looks lacy, crocheted or knitted, and it can be used detached, where it creates its own fabric.

It can be worked on a surface or into itself, you can create changes in patterns and texture by the direction you work it.

What is there not to like about a stitch that allows you to do all you want with it? To construct surfaces or forms that can be decorated, add detail and complement other surfaces, it can be used as a joining, interlacing technique. It can add rich texture and often transcend the tradition of how a stitch should look.

Detached buttonhole is a very old technique; many museum collections have magnificent examples in sixteenth-century whitework, where it makes high-relief forms. It can be used to create delicate insertion patterns or as a high-relief element that embellishes embroidery. Often worked over foundation threads, detached buttonhole stitch is worked on the surface without piercing the cloth or background stitching.

75 *Example of detached buttonhole stitch creating a form from a continuous line.*

BUILDING SURFACES: CONSTRUCTING OR CREATING A FABRIC FROM SCRATCH

Project 2. Child's bag

While this project is constructed entirely from buttonhole stitch, we will see later in the book how this stitch has also been used in conjunction with pompom flowers, tassels and edging projects. The poppy flowers have inspired the shape and surface of this bag. The detached buttonhole technique allows you to shape the form as you work row by row. Alternatively, you could work with circular knit or crochet to create this form. The little puff bag project is an ideal small bag for a young girl, and a lovely finishing touch to an outfit. Helen's mother, who often used the leftover fabric from home-made dresses to make matching drawstring bags, inspired this project. There are many super vintage bags available and aspects of these could provide inspiration for a new project or decoration.

The first thing to determine is exactly how wide and deep you want your bag to be, taking into account of the size of the hands you expect to go in and how much you want it to hold. The base of the bottom of the bag forms the anchor and starting point from where the stitches are worked. It is important that the base is strong, in the example shown, cardboard is cut accurately to the desired size, then sandwiched between a layer of felt on each side. The felt is oversewn together, allowing no slippage of cardboard or of the felt layers. Heavy denier tights are used to cover both sides of the base.

76 Left *Evening bag showing two types of beaded structure: top strip with a solid bead and a beaded fringe that loops round a constructed inner lining*. Right *Beaded bag with flower motif.*

As an alternative, if you wanted a softer pouch-type bag, you could do without the base, decreasing the buttonhole stitches until the tube comes to a point, which could then be decorated with a tassel or button detail.

For strength and for neatness a crocheted chain-stitch trim is made first, which needs to be the circumference of the base. This is then sewn with invisible thread to the edge of the base, or pinned to the base, which is removed when the buttonholing is done. From this secure line you start the buttonhole work; the example shown has the buttonhole stitch going into every second chain stitch.

Double-knitting wool is used doubled over to give a chunky look. It is best to have two balls to work from simultaneously. The stitch is worked all in one direction, hence the strong pattern created, it also gives the structure added stretch.

Unlike knitting, which uses a continuous yarn, for buttonhole stitch you have to cut a length of yarn first. To avoid a lot of knots, you will need to use much longer lengths of yarn than normally recommended when stitching (approx 2m). When you approach the end, instead of knotting you should introduce the next thread into the stitches. For a couple of stitches you will have double amounts of yarns as the one is used up and the other is being introduced. As you work creating a tube, it is very important to keep the tension even; this is difficult as the structure is soft and stretchy.

Stop when the bag is the depth you desire. The base inside and underside are also buttonholed. This is worked into the secure tight chain stitch that you first started with, again decreasing every other stitch as you work by skipping stitches until you are down to one in the centre. Turning the bag inside out, do the same inside, making sure your buttonhole stitch hooks onto the underside stitches.

A perfect solution for the lining is to use the top of a pair of heavy-denier tights. There is a channel through which a drawstring can be threaded; it also means there is no need for a pattern block or seams, except for the joining of the inner lining to the base board of the bag, using invisible thread. The other advantage is that the fabric adds to the stretch of the bag form; an appeal for a small bag.

BUILDING SURFACES: CONSTRUCTING OR CREATING A FABRIC FROM SCRATCH

This example has anchored the buttonholed trunk of the bag to the lining just under the channel for the drawstring. A finishing edging of frothy mohair represents the stamens of the poppy. The mohair yarn is doubled and is worked loosely. To the get the kinks and waves, increase by three or four stitches every third stitch. Unlike the trunk of the bag, where the stitch was continuous in one direction, the mohair 'stamens' are created back and forth, building up dense areas of stitches. In fact, you should aim to break up any pattern that might appear.

For the drawstring handles, it is important to use something smooth: a shiny cord, long laces, ribbon, or recycled leatherette straps from other bags or belts, as has been done here. You need two holes opposite each other in the channel for the drawstring. Make sure you have two long enough pieces of whatever you choose, so as not to restrict full opening of the bag aperture.

As stated, this whole bag uses only buttonhole stitch; even the small poppies at the end of the drawstring are buttonholed. Therefore the bag has different looks or qualities that the buttonhole shows: the pattern of one-direction buttonhole, the frothy organic, wavy structure and the poppy flower detail of the drawstring.

77 Base of bag showing how detached buttonhole stitch is built around an initial crocheted chain.

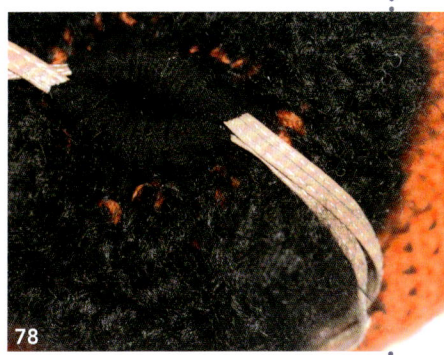

78 Detail showing drawstring opening. The lining cut from a pair of tights is flexible and requires no side seams.

79 The completed child's bag.

45

Decorating surfaces: embellishing an existing surface

5

Working with imagery

Beading

Beading is an ancient technique that is widely used in many cultures and historical periods. It is used to denote status or importance by its association with labour-intensive and time-consuming craftsmanship. Beading techniques can be used to make forms and structures, and can be used as decoration on a ground fabric. Beading has been used to transform the everyday, giving a rich couture finish to the overlooked and indistinguishable. Can you over-bead? Never! If you do not immediately see the impact, there is no point in beading at all. Even in a small detail like a button or a motif, beads should never be eked out or used so sparingly as not to be seen at first glance. For full dynamic

80 *Example of beading worked over folded/pleated fabric grounds.*

81 *Example of encrusted beading where we see the stretch fabric base the beads are attached to.*

DECORATING SURFACES: EMBELLISHING AN EXISTING SURFACE

effect and appreciation, beading should not only create a new visual effect, but should also change the weight and handle of an object. The embellishment and encrusting effect not only adds texture to a surface but makes an object glitter, shimmer and shine.

Sourcing materials

It is hard to create and design from poverty! Working from a meagre range doesn't allow for the excitement of unexpected contrasts. For best results, before embarking on any beading project it is worth amassing a good range of beads. Finding a rich range of suitable beads can be a challenge, but if over time you have collected a stockpile of beads it is much easier to augment what you have with specific buys as opposed to starting from scratch. Augmenting cheap beads with more expensive types will certainly reduce overall costs. It is important to build up your stock with a range of very small beads that can be added to by specialist quality beads to be used as highlights, extra texture and detailing. It is hard to fight the magpie in us all that wants to buy gorgeous beads, but for reasons of economy, these specialist purchases should only be made when there is a project in mind! The stock range of beads should build up a palette of specific colours with differences in scale, finish and cut. Finishes can range from matt, iridescent, pearlised, metallic and so forth, while cut can have a range of faceted, textured or shaped beads. Conventional beads can range from glass to plastic. By sourcing a wide variety you will have a rich palette of shades and tints to your colours. Subtle or dramatic variations of beads allow for a richer depth of field and create a lot more movement as the images or effects become more trompe l'oeil and less flat. Ultimately, to achieve couture desirability a selection of beads is indispensable.

Preparation

Beading does need time and adequate workspace to have everything to hand. When beading is for a 2D ground, it is best to stretch it in a hoop or frame then clamp this to a worktop, to allow for the use of two hands. This saves time and is especially applicable to big projects. For large images or expanses of beading, using a quilting frame will mean that you don't need to re-hoop over an area you have already beaded.

Binding a hoop
Delicate fabrics or pile fabrics such as velvet can often be damaged or marked by an embroidery hoop. One way to reduce damage is to wrap

82 *Variety of beads.*

83 *Treasure chest of beads.*

TEXTILE SURFACE MANIPULATION

long strips of cotton fabric or bias binding around the rings of the hoop. Use a white fabric so that there is no risk of dye transfer.

Needle and thread

You should always use good-quality fine strong thread, even invisible thread is sometimes best for beading. Do not be tempted to use cheap threads, as they snarl and unravel easily and with very little wear and tear the stitches will break. It would be distressing to spend all that time to have all your work come undone as a result of a cheap thread.

Another frustration is finding suitable needles. It is important when using the smallest of beads that you use the finest of beading needles. They must have a fine point (if too blunt, the needle creates too big a hole and your bead can go through the fabric).

Lighting

For such detailed and painstaking work you should make sure you are in a well-lit environment. This might be at a window, with a spotlight, or you may even need a magnifying glass! Make sure you always know where the needle is. Good practice means never leaving needles lying around or pinned into your clothing, as such fine needles are very dangerous if one gets into your body. Pincushions are the answer.

Beading techniques used in these examples are one bead, or at most two (small) beads per stitch; often there is movement of beads within a stitch, which with wear and tear will break, but also putting on more beads per stitch means they will not sit evenly, and visually this is not good. For 2D or large areas of beading it is suggested you make a double backstitch as an anchor. This will prevent unravelling if a thread does break (as can be experienced with cheap mass-produced machine-beading).

Transferring the image

If there is an image on a 2D surface you should draw an outline before beading starts. If this is on a white ground or precious fabric, the outline could first be done by tracing around a paper stencil using a small running stitch or backstitch. Never use felt-tip, as it bleeds; do not use a biro, as it can never be totally concealed. A pencil, unless hard-leaded, will leave a grubby halo. There are different pencils out there that have differing degrees of success, but just think about how you are getting image to fabric before you start. On dark fabrics you can draw a

84

84 *Linen thread and selection of beading, darning and upholstery needles.*

DECORATING SURFACES: EMBELLISHING AN EXISTING SURFACE

permanent outline by using a transfer technique: trace a mirrored outline onto greaseproof paper with a metallic marker, turn the paper over and place directly onto the right side of the fabric. Press with a cool iron and the marker will lift from the paper and transfer to the fabric.

Placement

Working with small patches or fragments on a light fabric allows you more flexibility in applying the motifs onto the finished garment. Cut the patches with a small 5mm excess of fabric, tuck this raw edge under the beading and use a slip stitch to attach the patch. Ensure that the beaded patches do not compromise the performance or construction of garment parts, or its handle or drape. This is important whether you work onto garment pattern pieces or onto an existing garment. Couture finishes will explore applying the beading over seams or even to disguise the seams. Working extra beading around the patches will allow the possibility of the beading trickling rather than having a hard edge.

In these samples you can see how free machine embroidery acts as a ground, to which the addition of beading can create luscious surfaces.

Sequins

Sequins are often used for large expanses as they allow for softer drape and feel than solid areas of beads. They can be used in ready-made trims, lines or individually. Sequins can be applied in one of two ways: a seed method to anchor individual sequins, or a fish-scale technique where the thread is covered by the application of the next sequin.

Like beading, applying sequins by hand is a technique we associate with rich embellishment and luxury. Embellishments come in and out of fashion, often coinciding with better economic times. Think of the Roaring 1920s, or of the late 1950s and early 60s with the expansion of industrialisation/urbanism and above all mass-produced consumerism. During the decadent 80s, sequin-encrusted decoration reached heady heights of luxury with Lesage's haute-couture collection for Versace. Van Gogh's inspired *Sunflowers* and his sculptured forms of foliage and grapes were all executed in the fish-scale sequin technique. Ironically, at present beading can be produced very cheaply in India and these surfaces are ubiquitous in high-street shops at a price that allows the masses to have what was once exclusive to the few, in defiance of the austere recession climate.

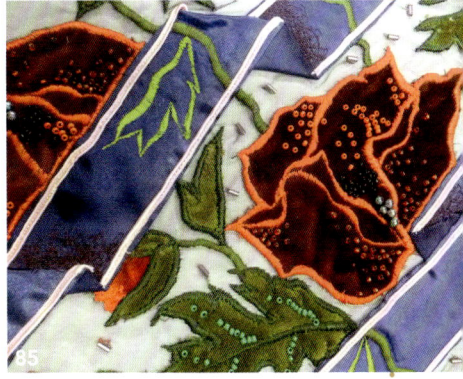

85 *Ribbon and velvet appliquéd on a transparent fabric with additional beading.*

86 *Detail showing machine ground and beading over a lace edge.*

TEXTILE SURFACE MANIPULATION

87 *Vintage 1960s embellished knitwear.*

More often than not, we use sequins with beads, but sequins used on their own have a very different look. Indeed, technically sequins require more planning and designing before you start. In the examples of beading shown in this book, imagery and texture can have a more organic style of construction. With beads we can even use wire to create high-relief effects, but the fish-scale sequin technique has none of this arbitrary placement, instead the sequins have to be systematically sewn down.

Fish-scale technique

This method is particularly useful for covering a solid area and relies on overlapping the sequins like fish scales. As you work from one side of the design to the other you bring the thread through the centre and down the outside edge that will be overlapped by the next sequin.

A fish-scale sequin surface can show clever, subtle imagery. When limited by just one colour and type of sequin, depending on the layered direction of the sequins, textures, tones and imagery appear. This can create wonderful optical illusions, always changing with light and movement. The articulation of the surface is fully realised when there is movement and play of light, as it reflects off the surface. This technique was used a lot in the 50s and 60s on knitted tops and cardigans.

The biggest challenge to applying sequins is getting a good range of materials to begin with. As previously mentioned, beads can be hard to find, but sequins are even more difficult. Recycled garments and jewellery are a good source for both beads and sequins, in which

88 *Fish-scale detail.*

DECORATING SURFACES: EMBELLISHING AN EXISTING SURFACE

case, all you need is time to unpick to acquire your new stock. If you are working with more than one colour, the range needs to allow for blending, so look for hints and tints of a colour. Blending flat colour with a matt or mother-of-pearl finish can help produce subtle effects.

The sequin projects show sequins used with beads (flat), with spangle sequins (faceted) and fish-scale sequins, a technique that needs a good quality sequin; not just for colour, but to ensure the hole is always in the centre of the disc (which is not always the case with cheap sequins).

Much of the preparation for applying sequins on a flat ground is the same as for beading, but the fish-scale technique does require some planning (and maybe sampling if never attempted before). For our poppy motif, sequins need to be layered in a way that creates directional movement of the petals. It is important to establish where you will start a motif and where your last sequin will be. Stitches must be consistent, so that you actually never see the hole of one sequin as the next lies over it, essentially you see only a crescent of each sequin (you will need a lot!). For the fish-scale technique, it is best to use the spangle-faceted type, even if augmented with the flat-disc type. The faceted type sits up proud of the previous sequin, creating relief and giving a greater depth of field and tonal change. Again, it is important to understand and visualise this, as a sequin that does not sit correctly in the sequence can really throw out the effect. It is difficult to correct a mistake in the direction of a sequin if not spotted at the time of stitching.

89 *Vintage sample showing the fish-scale sequin technique used to create rhythms, using matt and mother-of-pearl pink sequins. The change of direction ensures the facets capture the light to dynamic effect.*

90 *Fish-scale detail.*

TEXTILE SURFACE MANIPULATION

Project 3. Shirt with applied sequin motif

Often we find 'pre-loved' or second-hand items that have a flaw or stain that makes them unwearable. These can be great items to rescue with embroidered decoration. You can work on a separate voile ground so that the completed motif can be cut out and applied to a garment. This was the method used for this shirt project. Matching the colour of the voile to the shirt makes the task much easier.

Alternatively, you may want to work directly onto the garment (if it is lined, you will need to deconstruct), but try to stay away from too many seams as you still need to use a hoop for sequins. The voile technique might be best if you want sequins located over the shoulder, for example.

You may prefer the construction method used for the jacket project in image 93, where the petal shapes are made separately. These petals have a machine-embroidered edge, which gives them added definition and allows the petals to be self-supporting for a 3D effect. This can be reinforced if petals are to hang off edges. For a neat edge and to make edges less likely to fray when sewing, a cotton yarn is used, trapped under your free machining zigzag or satin stitch. Once the petals are made, they need to be worked in a hoop. Either use a fine net ground that can be easily cut away, or 'sew and tear' in a small hoop. While beading is quicker using the two-handed technique, it can still be done with one hand holding the hoop and the other doing the beading, but sequins definitely need both hands plus a hoop secured to a table top.

Once the petal-shaped sequins have been completed, you can construct your poppy. This method allows the repositioning and twisting of petals for better effects. The units mean you can take away or add more if need be, and do not involve the scary commitment of having the final design worked out beforehand when working directly on the ground (as with the shirt). For the jacket, attaching the elements means this can be worked over seams with only the beads of the stem having to be worked directly over seams, allowing the poppy head to be as 3D as you like. In fact, you could pad between the petals, if you wanted an even bolder statement!

Working with an existing structure, grid or mesh

These projects explore a contemporary interpretation of traditional counted-thread embroidery also known as canvas work. These use a grid and simple stitches to create surfaces with pattern and texture rather than imagery. Going back to basic principles, we take the position that

91 Shirt with appliqué of sequin motif. Photography by Philip White. Model: Polina Yakobson.

92 Detail of sequins on shirt.

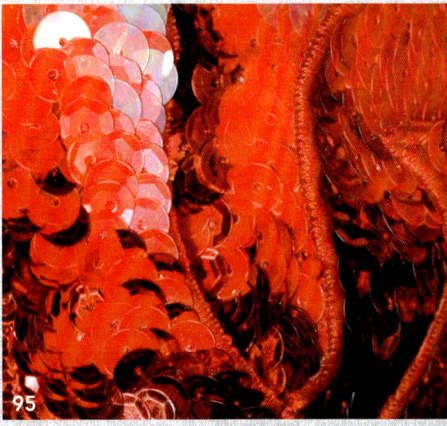

93 Appliqué on tuxedo jacket. Photography by Philip White. Model: Polina Yakobson.

94 Appliqué on tuxedo (detail).

95 Detail of 3D beaded petals.

96 Left *Pattern and colour exploration inspired by California wild poppy*, Papaver heterophyllum. Right *Assorted plastic baskets with cable-tie decoration.*

this technique is about adding to an existing grid or mesh structure, so instead of the classic Aida canvas, why not explore grounds such as metal cooling racks, garden ornaments, metal garden chairs, or even plastic laundry baskets?

Surfaces with tufts and loops

Crafts that were once common have now become a novelty to a society obsessed with technology. Whole generations used to rely on rag rugs and hand-knotted rugs made from scraps of fabric and reclaimed wool as essential interior objects. The activity of making has its own place in our collective cultural heritage.

Inspired by the cluster of stamens around the seed capsule in many of the poppies, we have been led to explore the possibilities of creating texture through spikes, tufts and loops in unconventional materials. There are many stitches and knotting techniques that create pile. The simplest is just to make a single stitch using a short length of thread and knot its two ends together. There are more formal approaches. Velvet stitch is one traditional canvas-work stitch that traps a loop under a simple cross stitch, and replicates the look of a hand-knotted carpet pile. By working these stitches in lines or blocks an all-over surface can be created and either left as a loop or cut to form a tuft. A shiny, high-twist yarn will give a different effect to a soft woollen tapestry yarn. Using many threads at the same time will produce a bulkier surface. We can exaggerate these techniques with longer loops in less rigid materials to create a dense, floppy pile.

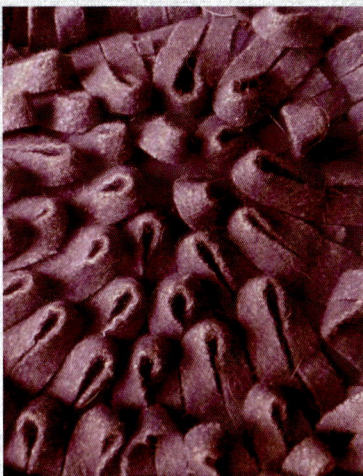

97 Left Papaver laciniatum. Right *Translation with raw edge strips of wool looped and sewn in concentric circles.*

98 *Velvet stitch worked on traditional Aida canvas.*

99 *Velvet stitch worked with clothes line on a plastic waste bin.*

100 Left *Photo of details of peony poppy.* Right *Sample of looped strips of wool on an upcycled reconstructed sheepskin jacket from the graduate collection of Paddy Rooney.*

TEXTILE SURFACE MANIPULATION

When we look at the poppies themselves, the blooms can be very formal. By pulling the petals apart we see the possibility of a much looser surface. Vintage embroidery using raffia with long and short stitch can also create rich surfaces. Cotton bias binding has a certain starched stiffness. It makes a great alternative yarn as the pre-folded edges give a clean, crisp quality; it is light and comes in many colours.

We can arrange the small folds of binding to create complex surfaces. Though expensive when bought in short lengths, an entire 25m roll can be bought relatively cheaply from a wholesaler.

Looped structures

The more structured poppies such as the corn poppy offer inspiration for another way of using bias binding to make a flower. For each of the four petals, take a 3m length of narrow bias binding. Fold this strip along the centre with the raw edges inwards. Crease along this entire length by pinching between your fingers and pulling taut. The starch in the binding will hold this crease relatively successfully. Then, starting

101 *Raffia embroidery on canvas bag.*

102 *Two different approaches to creating a tufted fabric using loops of bias binding stitched onto a ground.*

DECORATING SURFACES: EMBELLISHING AN EXISTING SURFACE

at one end, fold the length backwards and forwards in a zigzag with each fold about 10cm long. Use a needle and thread to attach each fold to the previous fold, creating a fan shape. At this stage the form tends to sprawl and is hard to contain. Now take another length of bias binding about 35cm long. Crease down the centre as before and sew the raw edge to the other folds. This will form the outside of the petal. Use a single thread to attach the fold to this outside line at key points. The spacing of these points will define the petal shape. Attach the end of the binding to the base of the zigzag folds. You now have your first petal. Repeat to make three more petals. Attach the four centres together to create a flower, making sure you attach all four with the crease edge on the same side of the poppy. You will need to sew the first few centimetres of each side of the petal to the next to give it more structure. To give the poppy more shape you can work from the back, gathering the edges of each fold, stitch by stitch, edge to edge in a tight spiral about 2cm from the centre. This will create a dip on the right side of the petal. If you are making a number of flowers, this gathering will ensure that each one has a slightly different attitude.

103 *Corn poppy and bias flower interpretation.*

104 *The bias flower, showing back and side view.*

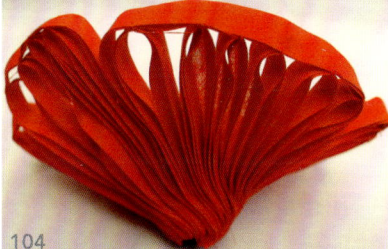

TEXTILE SURFACE MANIPULATION

To complete the flower, use the previous technique to create another centre from coils and ties, or gather a circle of fabric to create a sphere and stuff this before knotting off. This can be beaded to create a glistening centre.

Continuous loops

When exploring a theme we constantly look for visual connections. Responding to the twisted ribbon parcel bows in image 105, we can adapt this idea with bias binding. The ribbon is simply twisted backwards and forwards, but it can be a bit unwieldy to manage an even length of each fold and a good balance of direction. To help in this process we made a simple device from a sheet of scrap plywood. Hammer in a long skinny nail from the back so that there is a spike in the centre of the board. Tying on a pen with a piece of string, we can trace out a circle as a guide. Beginning with a short tail, push the binding onto the spike, taking great care not to stab yourself! Stretch the binding to the circle and hold down with your finger while you bring it back and push it onto the spike. Make sure the binding has formed a loop. These can have a twist or not, as you choose, but try to be consistent with each fold. Continue from one side of the circle to the other, slightly turning each time in a clockwise direction till you

105a Far left *Front and back view of a gift-wrap bow.* Left *Wooden board with nail used as a template to create loops for bias flower.*

105b Right top *Finished flower with centre of coiled bias and cable ties.*

have filled the entire circle. You can end here, but if you want a denser flower then continue to make another row. This can be of the same length or slightly shorter. You could also change colour at this point, for a variegated flower. When you are happy with your flower, cut the binding off with a short tail in the centre of the flower. Using a strong thread in a matching colour, prepare a needle ready to sew. Gently remove the flower from the spike. Ensure you keep a tight hold of it, or all your hard work will be undone! Use your prepared thread to sew through the centre of the flower with a few discreet backstitches and knot on the back.

To complete the flower you need to make the seed head. Simply coil a length of bias binding. This could be a single colour or a number of shorter lengths in gradated colour. Sew the raw edge down with a few tiny stitches. Then, using a contrast thread, knot the thread into the base with a backstitch, then wrap the coil by sewing through the middle hole of the coil and spacing the stitches to replicate the radiating lines of the poppy. When you are finished, gently push up the centre of the coil to create a more rounded shape.

For more contrast you might find working over plastic middles to be effective. These came from the centre of the spools of binding, but you could use plastic bottle tops, lids or tubes. You may need to pierce the centres but this depends on what you find.

106 Top *Exploration of flower centres using found plastic tubes and cable ties.* Bottom *Detail of flower centre with two colours of bias coiled and pushed up. These are wrapped with threads and surrounded by cable ties.*

TEXTILE SURFACE MANIPULATION

Zigzags

The bias flowers we have created are decorative elements that can be applied to any number of objects to add relief. Another simple technique is one that is often worked with paper, the zigzag. It relies on folding a strip in two, then folding each end over the other to create a spring.

Starting with a 25cm length of bias binding we can fold the strip and then pinch together to create a compact cube. When we have done this we can join the two ends together to create a star flower form.

107 Top left *Initial fold in centre of bias length, made at right angles.* Top right *Strip is turned over to create the second fold.* Bottom left *These two stages are repeated to create a folded length.* Bottom right *Completed folded strip is curled round to create flower form.*

Using multiple elements to create a surface

One symbol of balmy summer days would be the straw hat. The light structure with a large floppy brim provides welcome shade and has long been a vehicle for whimsical and pretty decoration. One obvious interpretation of the traditional canvas fabric is the loose weave of a straw hat.

You could buy a new hat, strip the decoration off an old hat or add to what is already there. The successful straw hat relies on a satisfying distribution of these three-dimensional elements. To achieve a pleasing end result, decide on a focal point to the left or right of the centre front and work out from here. This is the place for your bias flower, as it is the largest element and will command attention. The smaller zigzag flowers are best placed moving from a tightly clustered group to a more scattered distribution.

108 *Straw hat decorated with zigzags and a bias flower.*

109 *Details of hat decoration.*

Project 4. Upcycled garden chair

For this project we found a pale pink garden chair and used a range of different coloured bias binding.

This chair used eight spools of varying harmonious shades of lilac, pink and purple, and a single spool of orange cotton narrow bias binding.

There are many types of folding metal garden chairs that have a mesh or perforated back panel. These can act as a perfect ground for a multitude of tufts.

Cut the binding into about 20cm lengths. The pattern of the tufts is quite arbitrary, but what is important is to start in the middle and work each side alternately so you don't lose track of the pattern and can make sure it is symmetrical.

For the matching cushion, use the leftover lengths of the different bias bindings and apply them to a simple cotton fabric to create circular flower motifs that cover the entire cushion. These can be worked in two opposite versions, either working from the centre out, or from the outside in.

110 Top *Sketchbook page showing chair ideas with coordinating cushions.* Bottom left *Papaver laciniatum.* As the petals fall we see the structure of the poppy. Bottom right *Translation of the petals using bias binding knotted through a metal grid.*

111 *Two views of the folding garden chair.*

DECORATING SURFACES: EMBELLISHING AN EXISTING SURFACE

To create these you need a square of base fabric – remember you will see this, so use a sympathetic colour or print. A quilter's 'fat quarter' is ideal.

First, we will talk about the version that starts in the centre. Cut the entire 25m roll of binding into 12cm pieces, fold each one in half to establish the middle, and then again from both sides to create the arrow point fold. These form the petals and you should prepare all of these before starting. Remember to ensure the folds are identical with the raw edge either on the top or bottom of the petal. Either is fine but you will want your flower to be consistent.

With a pencil, lightly draw your starting circle in the centre of the square of fabric. For a dense flower the diameter should be smaller than the length of bias strip (about 10cm). This will mean that each petal overlaps in the middle and pushes up. For an open centre, make this circle larger. Using the sewing machine and a normal stitch, sew over the light pencil mark to establish your starting point as the first guideline. Take a petal and place the raw edges along the guideline. Use the machine foot as a guide to ensure your stitched line is even. Machine each petal in place. Ensure the edges are together and at right angles to the line, pointing inwards to the centre of the circle. You can choose to overlap the raw edges to create a sharper petal. Working from left to right, place the next petal evenly and machine it in place. Repeat till you have completed the first row. For the next concentric circle, machine another circle guideline 2cm out from the last one. Complete this row and repeat till you have created the flower. Place the raw edges along the guideline of stitching, with the loop end towards the raw edge of the base fabric.

To create different effects you can use a different colour for each row, vary the distance between rows and alternate the twists of petals facing up or down.

112 Top *First row of loops facing in.* Bottom *First row of loops facing out.*

113 *Flower made from concentric loops facing in. Starting from inner circle facing inwards, working outwards.*

114 *Flower made from concentric loops facing out. Starting from outside circle, working inwards.*

63

For the outward circle example, begin as before but with a circle about 10cm smaller than the square of fabric. Starting on the outermost circle, use the guideline of stitching to place each loop of binding. This time let the petal face outwards towards the raw edge of the base fabric. As before, work from left to right, sewing the raw edges along the guideline of stitching.

Reinterpreting soft folds and loops as spikes

These folds and petals are all very soft and feminine. If we look back at our starting point of the stamens, they are far more spiky and masculine.

Going back to the inspiration sketchbooks allows us to consider other materials. Close-up sections of leaves and the point where the stem joins the seed head show some quite brutal spikes and textures. Inspiration can come from unlikely sources. A child's pocket pop-up hairbrush seen from various angles looks at repetition and spikes. Visual similarities can be observed in a moulded latex swimming hat, or even close-up details of the bristles from worn-out yard brooms (see images 118 to 120). All have clusters of wayward spikes.

In our sketchbook pages we began to consider other containers that could be decorated and form the basis of ideas for alternative uses for the canvas technique (see images 121 to 123).

To demonstrate that there are several ways to apply spikes or tufts, we have looked at contrasting plastic cable ties with metal structures. This project is simple and fun. The yellow horned poppy (see image 121) inhabits Mediterranean coastal areas and gets its name from its long, slender fruits.

As you can see from the design pages we have explored other outcomes for this technique. Whether it is a laundry clothes peg basket or a garden hanging basket, all have a potential for upcycling.

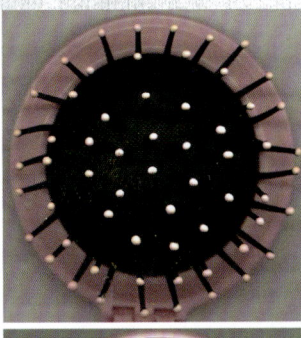

115 Inspiration sketchbook page looking at poppy stamens and materials.

116 Close-up detail of the texture underneath the seed head.

117 Inspiration can come from unlikely sources. A child's pocket pop-up hairbrush seen from various angles looks at repetition and spikes.

118

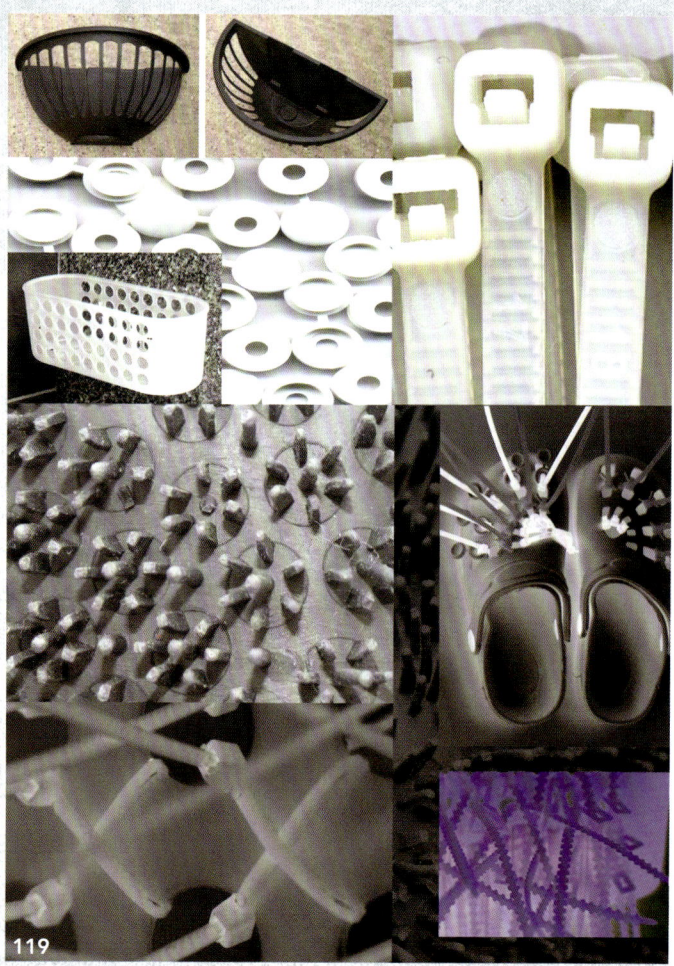

119

118 *Details of bristles from worn-out yard brooms, looking at clusters of spikes.*

119 *Sketchbook page of ideas for alternative uses for canvas-work technique.*

120 Left *Inspiration from moulded latex swimming hat.* Right *Various samples of cable tent stitch techniques.*

120

121 Initial design research board exploring translating the spikes of yellow horned poppy.

122 Shower tidy with garden ties.

123 Clothes-peg basket with black and white cable ties.

TEXTILE SURFACE MANIPULATION

Project 5. Child's chair and side table

The chair originally came with a back and seat of rainbow-coloured woven polyethylene. The first stage is to cut this away to get back to the clean, white, metal frame. Using a fine, bright orange polypropylene rope clothes line, wrap parts of the legs and sides and back frame. Use adhesive tape to hold the clothes line in place and wrap over this with a tight, even twist so that the tape is covered. Use a simple buttonhole stitch with short thread lengths, joining with a tight knot and trapping the raw ends under the wrapping as you go along.

With careful planning you should be able to work around the chair, hiding the majority of the joins. When you finish, knot into the buttonhole loop. If the wrapping gets too separated, you can work over with another layer.

The back and seat are two panels from shelf inserts. These came in white powder-coated metal. We chose them as they had an interesting arrangement of perforations.

Before attaching these, embellish with cable ties. Working from underneath, push up the cable tie through one hole and come down through an adjacent hole before pulling the tie taut. This leaves a

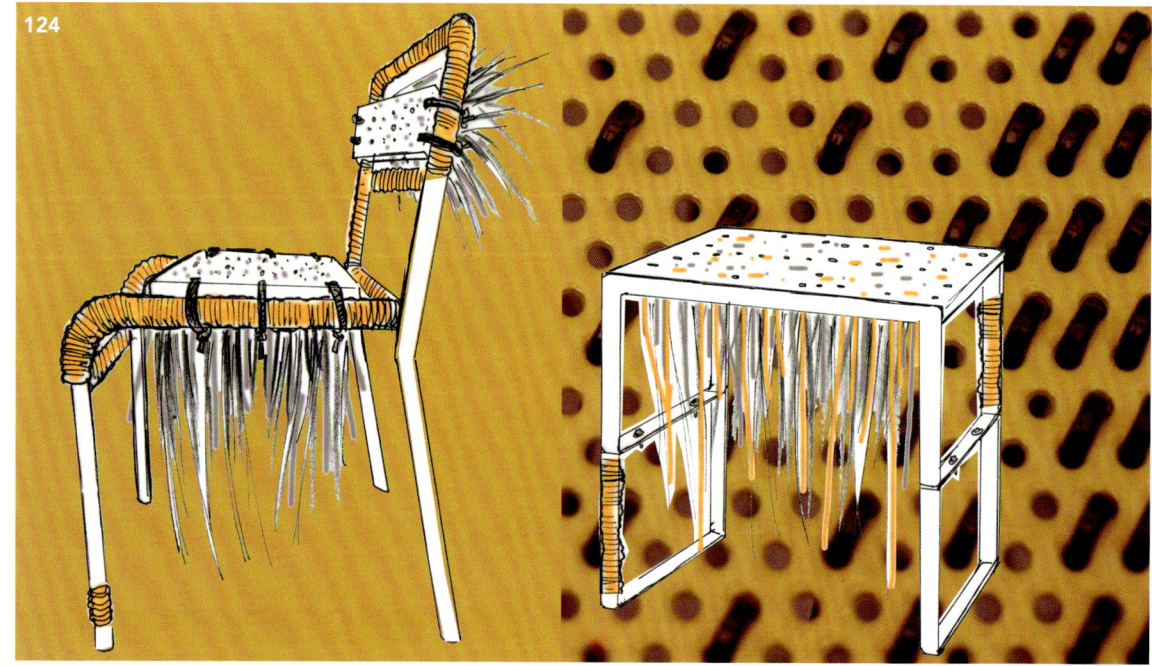

124 *Sketchbook development page of shelf side table.*

125 Detail of cable-tie decoration over orange silicon pot trivet.

126 Child's chair and side table.

127 Details of yellow powder-coated metal side table with canvas-work decoration in black cable ties.

128 Details of side table with canvas-work decoration.

TEXTILE SURFACE MANIPULATION

dramatic spike underneath and a neat stitch on the right side. Attach the back and side with more cable ties, but coming up through the shelf insert and wrapping around the frame itself before closing back on the shelf. As a finishing touch, use some much smaller cable ties to keep the orange wrapping in place.

For the matching stool or side table, make another of the tufted shelves. The shelf unit used for the chair panels came with attachable legs; both sets of these were used to create a better height (see image 126).

We found many different styles of metal side tables with perforated tops as we looked around the high-street stores for alternatives. This striking yellow table has holes that just fit the narrow cable ties. Rather than working every part of the surface, we have explored leaving spaces (see images 127 and 128).

Canvas work

Traditionally, this technique allows for the creation of images or patterns, requiring a regular grid of holes to allow for the use of counted-thread stitch techniques. Early examples of the technique used small stitches in one direction, over a single thread intersection, to replicate weave or tapestry techniques. This approach works best at delineating colour pattern or imagery, almost like pixels in a computer screen. Later developments, such as the European bargello, employed longer stitches that were worked over many thread intersections.

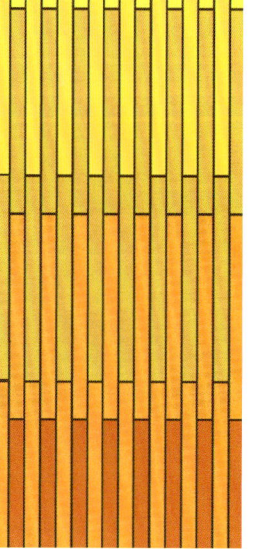

129 Top *Traditional canvas work to make an image*. Bottom *Canvas work technique to create bargello pattern.*

130 Left *Petal from California poppy showing colour gradation*. Right *Diagram showing how stitches are worked over several threads in a tightly packed parallel manner to create bargello-style colour blends.*

DECORATING SURFACES: EMBELLISHING AN EXISTING SURFACE

Tent stitch

The generic name for needlepoint canvas-work stitches is tent stitch. This is often used to fill in backgrounds or create flat areas for detail to stand out against. From the front, all variations look very similar, and it is only on the reverse that we appreciate the differences. With all three main types of tent stitch, each individual stitch is formed diagonally. The variations all depend on how you move from one stitch to the next, building rows or diagonal lines.

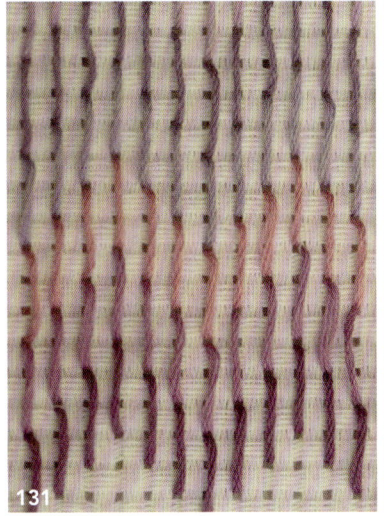
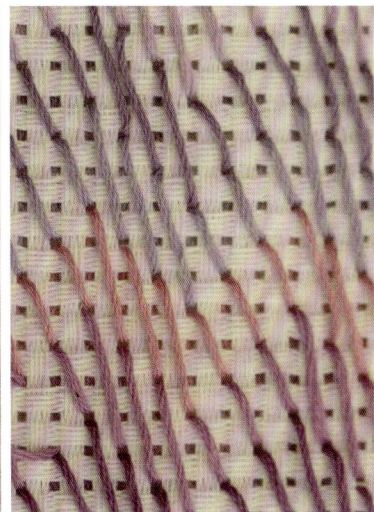

131 *Traditional bargello stitch on Aida canvas.*

The basic tent stitch has two notable versions: 'gobelin' when worked over several threads, or 'petit point' when worked on fine structures over a single thread. The most important consideration when choosing which way to form the stitch is what will happen on the reverse of your work. In these projects the back of the material is incredibly important, as the objects are unlined.

In describing how to do the techniques it is helpful to think of each stitch as covering an intersection of the canvas. If we use an unconventional grid we may also want to contrast this surface with the stitches and leave the ground with spaces or rest areas.

Basket weave is worked diagonally on the front, creating the opposite diagonal on the back. Of the three types this uses the greatest quantity of thread and creates a thick, durable surface on the back. It derives its name from this interlaced or 'basket' effect on the reverse.

Start in the top right corner of the area to be filled. To work the stitch, bring your needle up through the bottom left hole and insert the needle down the bottom right. Bring your needle up in the next hole to the diagonal upper left. Repeat the process, working upwards diagonally to form a row. The next row of stitches is worked in the opposite direction.

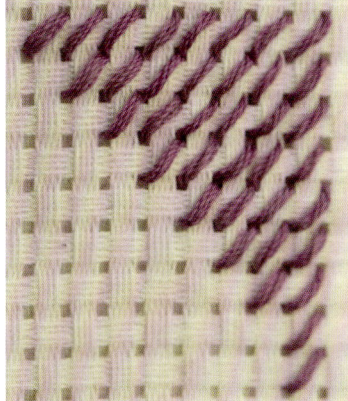
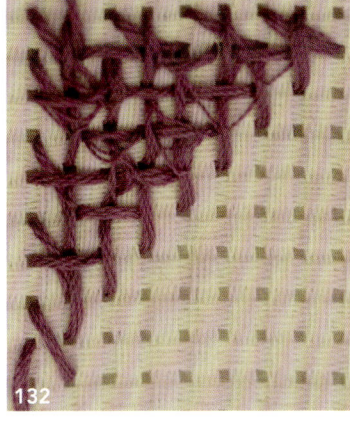

132 Top *Basket weave tent stitch front, worked from top left in diagonal rows.* Bottom *Basket weave tent stitch reverse.*

71

TEXTILE SURFACE MANIPULATION

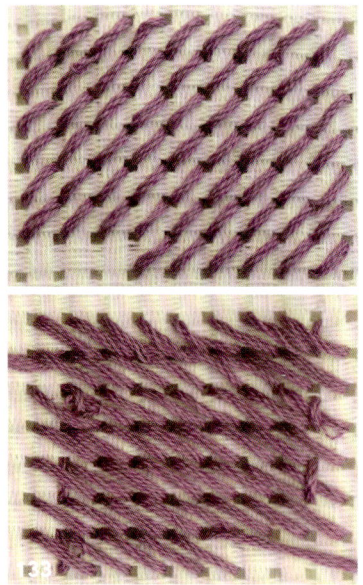
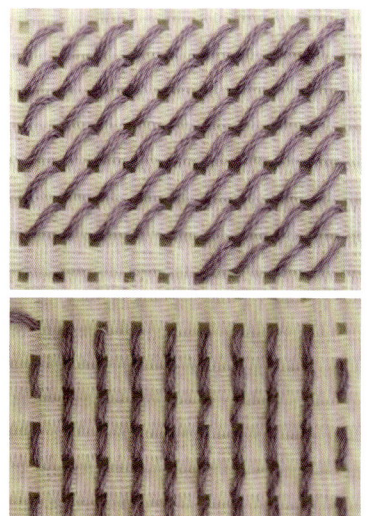

133 Top *Continental tent stitch front, worked right to left, top to bottom and reversing each row.* Bottom *Continental tent stitch reverse.*

134 Top *Half-cross tent stitch front, worked right to left, top to bottom and reversing each row.* Bottom *Half-cross tent stitch reverse.*

Continental tent stitch is worked horizontally. Start at the top right corner of the area to be filled. Work the first line from right to left and the second line from left to right. Every stitch formed from bottom left to top right over the threads. Reverse is thicker with stitches on the diagonal.

Half-cross tent stitch is worked horizontally line by line. Left to right on first line, with stitches bottom left to top right and then reversed on return coming back right to left with stitches from top right to bottom left. This has a definite 'right' side as it uses the least thread as the back of the work crosses only one thread. The back side can be quite mean-looking with only a horizontal thread. On more delicate canvas this stitch will cause a warping effect.

Plastic surfaces

In these projects, all manner of unconventional yarns from garden string to shredded T-shirt jersey can add a variety of textures. There is also the possibility of exploring texture contrast and leaving part of the grid exposed. Plastic bins often have regular holes or perforations that can be used as grids.

The bright, strong colours of the petals have been digitally manipulated using a simple dot pattern. This project is primarily about how effective a very simple technique can be when translated through unusual materials, changes in scale and strong use of colour.

135 Top *Three plastic bins with tent-stitch techniques worked in polypropylene clothes line.* Bottom *Details of tent-stitch techniques worked in polypropylene clothes line.*

136 Top *Inspiration with computerised image of petals and spots.* Bottom *Experiments with variations on tent stitch with chunky yarns.*

137 *Close-up of three variations of tent stitch using a composite thread made up of several strands of shredded T-shirts.*

TEXTILE SURFACE MANIPULATION

138

138 *Design sketchbook page showing ideas for pink baskets with shredded grey T-shirt yarns.*

Old T-shirts with a few stains or holes can make an amazing yarn. A macramé lark's head knot is the starting point of all macramé projects and is used here to create an over-sized layered fringe. Shredding or carefully cutting will give different qualities this kind of yarn.

To make the yarn from old T-shirts, try and find one that is a tubular knit (no side seams), which you can cut in a continuous strip. Obviously you can do the same on T-shirts that have side seams, but the resulting yarn won't be as smooth. The seams may add a texture detail that you will want to exploit.

Project 6. Laundry basket

This method of updating canvas work worked on unconventional grids or meshes with unusual materials can realise a number of simple and effective products. Many discount stores sell a plethora of plastic laundry baskets with perforated surfaces. These come in a range of fun colours and often reflect contemporary trends

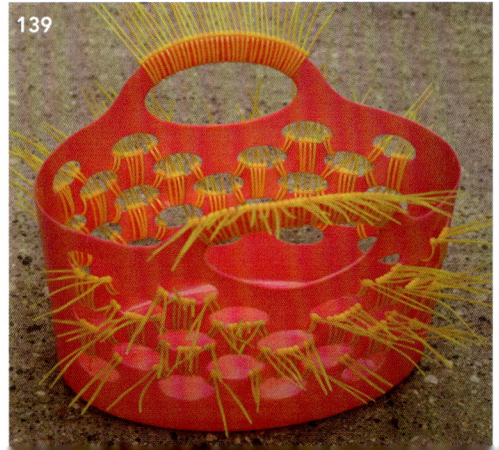

139 *Two plastic baskets worked with different colour combinations and canvas work cable-tie techniques.*

DECORATING SURFACES: EMBELLISHING AN EXISTING SURFACE

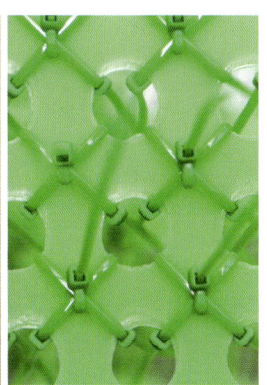

We can also find plastic clothes-peg baskets, which have regular holes that can be used for canvas-work stitches. We can create a parody of a cross-stitch surface, with extra ties added as a wrapping stitch. For extra height and drama we can thread a number of cable ties onto a single tie and then pull into a loop. Having established the direction of these products, it was time to reconsider colour. This example used an image of a fading corn poppy to decide upon a colour palette.

Rhodes stitch

Rhodes stitch creates a textured star unit, almost like a stud. The thread is sewn round and around a central point. It can be worked individually or in rows or blocks. The stitch is worked with long spokes overlapping a central point.

With Rhodes stitch you need to consider where you want the last stitch to fall, as this is the one on the top and the most raised. Normally this is a vertical stitch. To ensure this you need to start one diagonal clockwise from this and keep working in the same direction till the square is filled.

When looking at the heart-shaped petals of a particular poppy we are reminded of the shape of a love heart. Rhodes stitch can also be worked over shapes such as a heart or star.

Securing ends
When working with bold, chunky threads there are always issues about how to start or finish in a tidy and secure way. The method used depends on how pliable the threads are, or how stable (they can easily fray or unravel).

140 *Plastic clothes-peg basket; ties are worked to make cross stitch variations.*

141 *Detail of cable ties threaded onto another tie and pulled into a loop.*

142 Top *Inspiration for the Rhodes stitch 'stud' effect from a scan of the underneath of an opium poppy.* Bottom *Translation as Rhodes stitch worked with upholstery braid on plastic canvas.*

TEXTILE SURFACE MANIPULATION

143

In most cases we suggest that you start by leaving a length of thread that can be tucked into the stitches at the end. To be really durable these can be secured with a discreet backstitch with a polyester sewing thread. A plastic bag provides a tube that can be cut in a continuous, circular bias strip.

We experimented with a very large laundry basket – a perfect ground for the canvas-work stitches – worked with a Rhodes stitch square and heart in shredded pink plastic. The background is stitched in T-shirt jersey. Knotted and wrapped upholstery cords are reminiscent of withered petals with pollen and coiled stamens.

The emphasis is on the yarns; let them do the work and keep the techniques simple and bold. Having sampled how composition can be explored through design and development, this shows the possibilities of tent stitch, velvet stitch and Rhodes stitch. We have used reclaimed upholstery braids to work the stitch on a large scale.

144

145

143 *Stages in working Rhodes stitch over a 4 x 4 grid.*

144 *Variations of Rhodes stitch worked with different materials over the same 6 x 6 grid.*

145 *Sketchbook page with scan of a heart-shaped petal, which was the inspiration for working Rhodes stitch in a motif shape. The scale is exaggerated and worked over a large laundry basket in pink plastic with a background of T-shirt jersey. The plastic yarn was made by cutting a tube of plastic diagonally to create a continuous strip, rather like peeling an apple. It was made from a bag sold for growing strawberries in hanging baskets*

  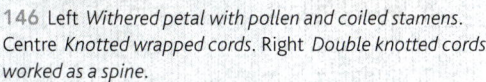

146 Left *Withered petal with pollen and coiled stamens.* Centre *Knotted wrapped cords.* Right *Double knotted cords worked as a spine.*

147 *Double knot in bias binding.*

148 *Design development page showing possibilities of tent stitch, velvet stitch and Rhodes stitch.*

149 *Close-up of basket detail worked with upholstery braid.*

150 *Finished basket.*

TEXTILE SURFACE MANIPULATION

Project 7. Child's clogs

Since the trend for plastic slip-on shoes began a few years ago, there has been any number of cheap versions of these on the high street. These are more often than not outgrown, worn out, or disposed of after a few months. This project is a simple one that could be done with children. Be careful that the ties are pulled tight and that there are no rough edges on the inside of the shoe. For the best effects, work into next-door holes rather than working over larger spaces where the ties will not be able to be pulled taut and will sag on the inside. Obviously if they are to be worn, you need to be aware of the practicalities of trailing spikes, but as a fun project there is endless scope for creativity.

The shoes come in a rainbow of different colours, emphasised by the selection and combination of other materials.

Applying the techniques of canvas work and simple cross stitch, we need to look at the object in the round, from front, back, side and top. Alternative possibilities for canvas work can use the cable tie as a thread, to trap or secure a 'bead' in place, in this case a tile spacer, or a plastic screw cap.

The cable ties can be bundled together and secured as a flourish or tassel.

151 *Experiments with three pairs of child's plastic clogs.*

152 Orange clogs with coiled cable ties.

153 Green clogs. Left *Using screw caps as sequins.* Right *Using tile spacers as a cross-stitch bead.*

154 Pink clog with coiled cable ties.

Manipulating: taking a surface and changing it through stitch

Quilting

Quilting is one way of laminating or combining layers of fabrics that traditionally attaches three layers of fabric with stitches or ties at various points. The middle layer, called wadding or batting, is often a soft insulating material. Stitches pass through all layers, pulling the layers together. The stitch provides a tension or pinch that flattens the area around it so the unstitched areas still appear raised. Stitches can be made in figurative running patterns, spots or geometric lines.

For these projects we have chosen to use digitally printed fabrics as a base for the quilting process. This allows the stitch to create surface pattern or reinforce imagery inherently in the fabric. Both these projects can be worked just as successfully on a plain coloured, woven pattern, jacquard or appliquéd fabric.

You can develop your own prints and get them printed at any one of a number of textile bureaus. This can be as simple as sending off an original digital photograph. Modern digital cameras can shoot at such high resolution that it is possible to print a large piece of cloth from a single image. For those who have knowledge of digital manipulations there are many software programs to help develop or modify imagery. Some of the commercial bureaus even have software that can turn an uploaded image into a repeat over a whole fabric length. Most of these companies are used to working with students or individuals and are happy to talk through any concerns you may have. The fabrics can be expensive, but it does give incredible creative control.

155 The bottom section shows the original image at high resolution where every detail is sharp. The top section shows how the quality of the image deteriorates as the DPI decreases.

Formatting

Working at the right digital size is one of the key factors in getting the result you want. Digital files are measured in DPI.

Dots per inch (DPI) is a measure of spatial printing or video dot density, in particular the number of individual dots that can be placed in a line within the span of 1 inch (2.54cm). The DPI sets a ratio of pixels within a specific area. When the image changes size, the number of pixels cannot change. So if the image gets bigger the pixels become cruder. When the image gets smaller, the pixels become sharper.

The human eye struggles to see the difference between anything finer than 150 to 180 DPI actual size, which is why most printers and outputting devices work at this ratio.

Fabric selection

A coarsely woven fabric such as a furnishing linen will struggle to capture really tiny marks or qualities. Sheer fabrics often wobble a bit when the fabric is coated and the end result can be slight curves to geometric patterns, so it is often a question of combining the right fabric with the right design.

Remember to print a bleed or hem in character with the rest of the fabric. Fabric is not paper; it may shrink slightly between print and processing, so if you can't afford the time or money to get samples printed (always recommended), then print about 5% bigger than you want the final fabric, or allow a reasonable hem around any pattern piece.

Differential shrinkage

This technique is worked over at least two, but normally three layers. The sandwich is made up of fabrics where the weave structure or yarn type will shrink differently at the same washing temperature. It relies on the free machine stitch to act as a resist that allows the properties of the layers to come into their own. The trick is to let the fabric do the work for you. In these samples we see how the middle layer of an open-weave cotton muslin shrinks, forcing the top layer to puff out. It creates a quilting effect that is soft and light.

Temporarily holding it together

Tacking is one part of the creative process that can seem quite dull. However, it is vital that you put the time into tacking the layers of the fabric sandwich together. Find a flat surface where the entire piece can be laid flat. Use the selvedges to help you get everything straight by ensuring all the layers' selvedges are parallel. Use pins to hold the layers in position while you tack. Use a thread of a similar colour or white thread. If working on white fabrics, don't use coloured thread for tacking, as there is a danger that the dye may contaminate the white fabric.

Work outwards from the centre with radiating straight lines, using a long running stitch and securing the first and last stitches with a backstitch.

Machine stitching

The sewing is worked on a domestic sewing machine with a free machine embroidery technique. The cardinal rule when using an embroidery hoop is that for hand work the stretched fabric is always at the top so the hand underneath can push upwards. With machine embroidery the stretched surface is flat at the bottom so it can be pressed onto the machine plate. The fabric is held taut on a bound hoop so that it has a slight bounce. Be careful not to pull the fabric off grain, as this will mean that the piece will not sit flat when it is removed from the ring.

Before committing to the real thing, test your machine tension. If the loops form underneath then your bottom tension is too tight or the top is too loose. If the loops appear at the top (a whip stitch), then your top tension is too tight, or your bottom tension is too loose.

Always begin with your feet off the foot control, and with your right hand manoeuvre the wheel to make a stitch by pulling up the bobbin thread through the fabric. If you do not do this, the excess bobbin thread may bunch up and create a thread lump or 'dead squirrel' on the reverse. This is poor craftsmanship and a disaster if worked on a sheer fabric. Use small stitches where possible. To do this, move the hoop slowly and run the machine at a higher speed. The slower you run the machine and the faster you move the hoop, the longer the stitch and consequently the greater likelihood of the needle breaking and causing fabric damage. With experience you will build a rapport with the rhythm of your machine and co-ordinate your pressure on the foot control with the speed you move the hoop.

Always keep your fingers well outside the hoop. Some machines have a special darning foot to apply pressure and stop the fabric bouncing and causing missed stitches. This is not always necessary and can impede your vision of the work. If not using any foot, always remember to place the pressure foot bar down or the machine will not create tension. If you are not using a foot, you should be more mindful of the exposed needle, exercising good practice whereby you keep your fingers on the outside edge of the hoop to guide and move the fabric.

Start in the middle of the fabric piece and work outwards in a radiating direction to avoid lumps. Always check the fabric is taut in the hoop and be careful not to catch the edges of the fabric underneath the hoop. If this happens you will probably have to cut the fabric from the machine and either find a way to repair or disguise the hole, or start again with a new piece.

Garments

It may be possible to buy a commercial pattern or to find an existing garment or object that has the right shape and fit. Then, you can to take the garment apart or lay it down flat and trace around the individual pattern pieces. Remember that existing or vintage garments may have shrunk, stretched or settled. Common sense should tell you which lines or part of the pattern piece shape should be straight and which should be symmetrical. Remember that left and right should mirror exactly and each edge of a pattern piece should align exactly with the piece it is to be sewn to. Corrections to what you have traced will be needed. Being clean, accurate and meticulous are essential.

TEXTILE SURFACE MANIPULATION

Sewing fabrics together

Those who don't have great dressmaking skills should seek help from someone more experienced. If you are cutting out pieces, remember that it is always advisable to 'check twice and cut once' – we have all cut two left sleeves or not allowed for the nap or pile of a fabric when cutting out different parts.

It is customary to make a prototype of your product. For a garment this is called a 'toile'. It is a chance to check fit and shape. When making this, it is important that the fabric you make it in relates to the weight, handle and performance of your real fabric. For instance, does it stretch? Is it light, medium or heavy weight? A toile is traditionally made from calico, which comes in different weights. It is cheap and you can try many versions before committing to your final fabric.

Be informed about how you expect the article to be made in an appropriate way for your customer or market level. For example, sheer fabrics look best when finished with a French seam, while heavy interior fabrics will need to be overlocked to prevent fraying. Ensure that the person you are asking to do this work for you has the necessary experience, available machinery and expertise to do the job.

Always ensure you have discussed the fee first. There is nothing worse than an awkward conversation when the job is over; it's far better to be up front and know what you are both letting yourselves in for.

Project 8. Woman's quilted jacket

This project is inspired by the mood and colour of a watercolour painting of an opium poppy. The warm, comforting colours had the potential to be realised as a loose jacket. Work began with an initial sketchbook page considering how the colour and pattern could be applied to a garment. The jacket is designed to exploit the soft blanket-like drape of the differential shrinkage method with the qualities of a lightweight, soft woollen twill. The jacket pattern is simple, with only five pieces and no darts or complex constructions. The pattern itself can be scaled up from the diagram shown. What is important is that the measurements relate to the size you want to make your jacket. It should be possible to find a commercial pattern for a similar unstructured unlined jacket, noting key measurements like arm length and centre back are the proportions you are interested in. It is highly recommended that you make a toile beforehand.

156 *Initial inspiration comes from a watercolour study of an opium poppy.*

157 Sketchbook page showing jacket design development.

158 Series of ideas exploring placement.

TEXTILE SURFACE MANIPULATION

159 *Diagram showing how the pattern pieces will be cut from individual engineered prints.*

160 *Detail of print design showing how the layers of pattern are combined.*

161 *Detail of stitched piece after washing.*

The pattern pieces will be cut from individual blocks of printed and quilted fabric. The digital prints are engineered to relate to the pattern pieces. The five pattern pieces are laid out (with cutting allowance) within the dimensions of the fabric to be printed. Ensure you keep the pieces on grain so that when you cut them out they will hang correctly. Remember you will need to leave at least 5cm at either selvedge so that the fabric can be printed. The digital bureau will advise on the exact tolerance they need. The separate pieces are created individually and then combined into a single digital file ready to be sent for printing. This final file will be too big to email. Some companies prefer you to send the file on a disc, while others have a facility for you to upload the file to a server where they can access it. For economic reasons the edges are filled with images that can be used for sampling and testing.

The desired effect is to take the opium poppy images with crawling insects and mix and match them over the garment, creating a patchwork look. The quilting stitches follow the imagery of the print.

MANIPULATING: TAKING A SURFACE AND CHANGING IT THROUGH STITCH

The bobbin thread colour is slightly darker than the lining fabric.

The differential shrinkage technique comes alive when the stitched layers of fabric have been washed.

This jacket is deliberately unlined. The lining is joined to the top fabric as part of the quilting process. Raw seams and edges are bound in a highlight colour, although alternatively they could be covered with a hand-worked blanket stitch for a more homespun look. This same type of jacket could be realised with plain, patchwork, bought prints or even hand-painted fabrics.

162 *Detail of stitched and shrunk fabric after washing.*

163 and 164 *Final jacket. Photography by Philip White. Model: Polina Yakobson.*

87

TEXTILE SURFACE MANIPULATION

Project 9. Quilted evening coat

The peony poppy has a wonderful sculptural quality. The petals that curl in multiple directions reminded us of a comforting, wrinkled surface and we imagined that, if produced on a huge scale, they would envelop the body like a duvet.

With this shrinkage quilting technique we let the fabric do the work! The stitching is a resist that stabilises the fabric and the inner layer shrinks so that the top layer puffs up. This is particularly effective if the top layer has a high shine or lustre. To develop the concept from an initial drawing we first scan the ink drawing at a high resolution and isolate the black marks as a separate layer. We can then manipulate these on the computer through CAD development, working with layers and differing scales of imagery.

The coat shape is a development from many traditional garments where there is little or no wastage from a rectangle of fabric. Very fitted clothes that involve many pattern pieces and complex cutting can end up torturing a beautiful fabric. We find it is often best to work with a simple shift or blocky shapes, where we can resolve the design in the cloth rather than with complex making. This coat can be made with zero waste – a term used by many eco or sustainable designers who see the fabric as something special and resent the waste that ensues.

165

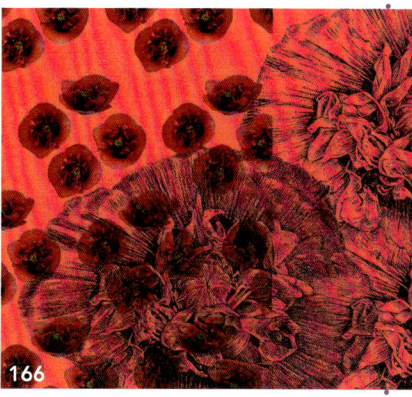

166

165 *Ink drawing of a double peony poppy.*

166 *Drawing and CAD development.*

167

167 *Sketchbook page showing variations of colour blocking and image layout.*

Using a computer as a means of experimenting with a multitude of design possibilities within an initial idea for a garment shape makes it easy to generate impressive notebook pages.

The body of the dress is a basic rectangle, the full width of the fabric and a length that is twice the length from shoulder to hem. The sleeves are two separate pieces that form tight, elongated cuffs.

You may not be designing for a size zero model but for someone who may be wider than tall, or who may have voluptuous curves. It is worth spending some time exploring proportion, creating an initial toile that balances the width and length of the garment in a way that is flattering for your customer.

From the illustration we can see how the design is prepared for printing and the layout showing how the pattern pieces of main body and sleeves fit within the selvedges.

168

169

168 *Design development, exploring proportion.*

169 *Sketchbook page showing possible layout for dress design and detail of print.*

TEXTILE SURFACE MANIPULATION

170 Top *Final print with areas cut away to create coat shape.* Bottom *Coat pinned together during development stage.*

The coat is printed on a sensuous silk satin with an unseen layer of cotton muslin and a lining of shocking pink silk habotai. It is light but very warm with a bouncy quilted nature. It not only drapes and slinks, it cuddles! The relaxed oversized style makes it perfect for an explosive colour statement on a fresh winter's day. It could also be worn with a belt for those who want a more defined waist

Kantha *and* sujini *quilting*

In this style of hand-stitched quilting, simple running stitches are worked through several layers of fine fabrics to create a rippled or slightly gathered effect. It has traditions in clothing as decorative edges on saris and also as a way of upcycling old garments to produce beautiful, lightweight quilts or blankets called *nakshi*. There are many scholarly books looking at the history of *kantha* and the use of traditional motifs. It is acknowledged that although it is popular throughout West Bengal and many parts of India, this technique is most commonly associated with Bangladesh.

171 and 172 *Final quilted coat back. Photography by Philip White. Model: Polina Yakobson.*

173 *Final quilted coat front, showing flash of lining. Photography by Philip White. Model: Polina Yakobson.*

TEXTILE SURFACE MANIPULATION

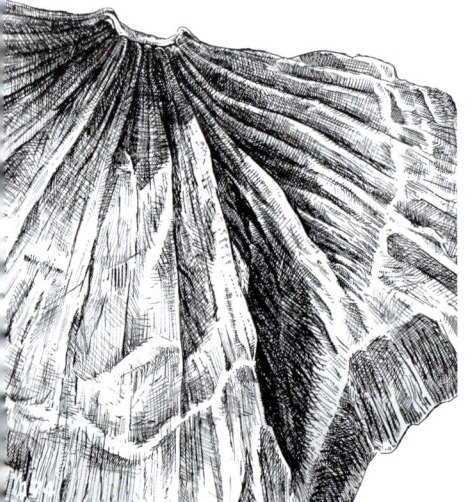

Sujini (sometimes spelt *sujani*) embroideries are part of a tradition from Bihar in north-east India. They are made by women and given to family members to celebrate weddings or births. Like *kantha*, they are worked over layers of old fabrics from saris and other clothes and are used to make quilts. They are similar to *kantha* in that they use running stitch and often have a narrative element, the main difference being that *sujini* do not have the rippled effect we see in *kantha*. Today community groups such as ADITHI take responsibility for the sustainability of such crafts and allow a creative means of expression for the women who make them.

In embroidery there are very few unique processes. We can see stitches as being flat, looped or knotted. Most are derived from the three simple ways of making a stitch:
- up and down – **running stitch**
- up and down with a wrapping movement – **stem stitch**
- looping – **buttonhole stitch**.

It is not surprising, then, that we can see similarities to these simple techniques in the Japanese *sashiko* ('little stabs') running-stitch quilting. The main difference is in the choice of base materials, colour and design pattern style, as the Japanese technique is more geometric, with more open areas that remain unstitched.

The other main consideration when working the stitches concerns the 'rivers' or unstitched spaces. The bits that are not stitched are the bits that puff up, so you need to stitch the recessive or shadow areas with darker tones or shading. By aligning the stitches you can create ridges

174 *Initial ink study of poppy petal, looking at ridges and ripples.*

175 *Manipulated drawing of petal and two samples of* kantha, *showing the ridges that the running stitch can form.*

MANIPULATING: TAKING A SURFACE AND CHANGING IT THROUGH STITCH

that have a soft, organic movement, forming a spiral, a chevron or even a zigzag. A brick repeat structure where each stitch is offset will ensure the fabric area is completely flat, as there are no large spaces to create ridges.

The petals of the oriental poppy have proved a fascinating inspiration. The ripples of the crinkled petals can be recreated through *kantha* stitch processes. To create more prominent ridges, pull the running stitches tight to gather the fabric. Great subtleties can be achieved just by considering the relationship between thread and ground.

Even on the same fabric, if we change the weight of thread, or use more than one strand, or vary the length of the stitches, the space between the stitches or the direction, we can see endless permutations. If we layer cotton net over a printed cotton base it will create a shadow effect in the ridges of the *kantha* pattern. This will also happen if you use a sheer fabric.

Referencing back to our initial source, we can observe the contrast of the circular seed head against the more relaxed ripples of the petals. We may work the fabric with parallel rows of set patterns on the machine to create a stitched grid to work over. You can also explore the differences of working with a dip-dyed thread over a flat colour or a solid colour thread worked over hand dip-dyed habotai silk. *Kantha* can be worked in a single direction or with movement such as spirals or diamonds that give a raised nipple-like effect. These can be very irregular and organic in feel, or more geometric using a square diamond stitch spiral. We can create gently striped effects by changing the colour of each column. In the samples you can see the effects of using different threads. Even with a stranded embroidery cotton the change from a single strand through to the full six gives a lot of subtle variety.

176 Sample showing how you can achieve very different effects by varying the number of strands of thread or the density of spacing.

177 Kantha *over a print on viscose satin. The shine on the fabric exaggerates the rhythms.*

MANIPULATING: TAKING A SURFACE AND CHANGING IT THROUGH STITCH

Project 10. Coordinating throw and cushions

In developing products for interiors we went back to the source and produced much looser drawings based on the radiating lines of the seed heads. We began sampling by considering using a ground of transfer print on viscose satin. The shine on the fabric exaggerates the rhythms of the quilting. An alternative would be to create a digital print on transparent chiffon, which is then layered over a cotton and worked with simple rhythms in running stitch.

Traditional *kantha* quilting is often worked through several layers of soft or fine fabric, and in this project we use a top layer of textured slub silk. This has a dry, papery effect and means that the print can't be too detailed. Initial inspiration came from the drama of this manipulated photograph from which we developed detailed drawings and manipulated in CAD.

The final digital print design for the throw was made of a number of large images that were simply repeated in a half-drop pattern. Contrast between these very textured areas and a simple flat ground that would not be stitched will help the final throw to fall and fold rather than being too solid. For the starting point of the cushions we looked at a high-resolution close-up scan of a compound pistil on the seed head. Every seed head is slightly different, with dramatic differences between the sub-species.

178 *A series of different approaches to* kantha.

179 Left *Photo of poppy petal.* Middle and right *Cotton net over a printed cotton base creates a shadow effect in the ridges of the* kantha *pattern.*

180 Left *Centre of a peony poppy.* Middle *Kantha worked in spiral to echo the shape of the seed head.* Right *Spiral formed to give raised effect.*

181 Top *Diagram of diamond pattern.* Bottom *Sample using square diamond stitch spiral.*

182 *Research page of photos and drawings of centre of seed head.*

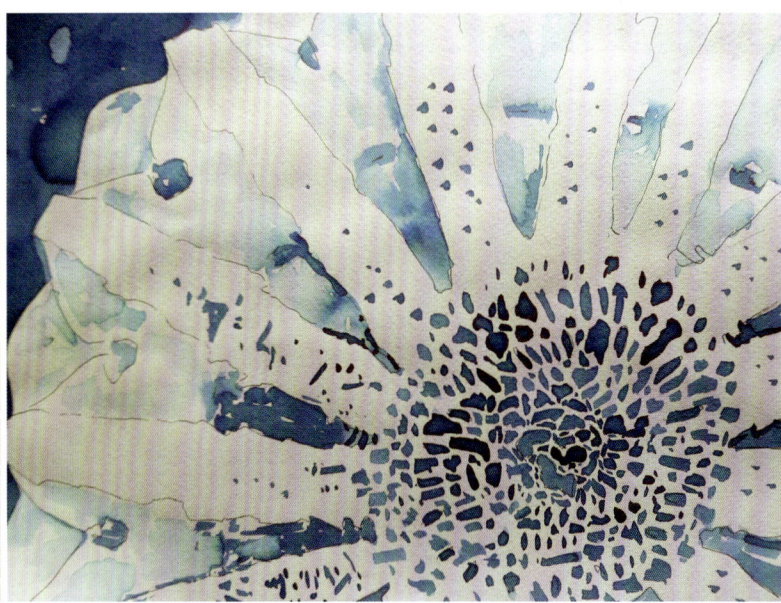

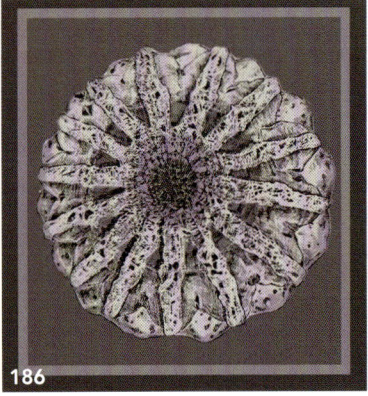

We decided to develop two similar but slightly different digital print designs for the cushion. The border is important; when working these there was more opportunity for exploring colour possibilities and detail. For the back layer of the throw we used a ready-made throw of wool/cashmere blend as a backing on which to apply the print layer before quilting. This has a slightly spongy quality. It means that the *kantha* will appear more ridged on the front, but on the reverse the stitches even out with a slightly indented or engraved feel. The centre of each flower is worked in a contrasting mint green thread to add a visual punch. A varied dip-dyed thread was used for the main part of the petals. This gives more life to the back of the throw.

As this is such a large product we tacked everything in place before machine-quilting around the main shapes. The nature of the technique means that the throw is reversible. The *kantha* technique creates a lot of movement with strange lumps and bumps as the stitches are worked in opposing directions. This preliminary work of temporarily holding the whole thing together, plus the permanent machine-stitched anchor points, makes the whole process more manageable. This quilt took about 150 hours of hand stitching. For the cushions we used a backing of wool tweed, as this will not be seen in the final product. The quilted panels are mounted onto pre-made cushions.

183 *Scan of compound pistil on seed head.*

184 *Initial inspiration with manipulated photograph.*

185 *Digital print design for throw.*

186 *Digital print design for both cushions.*

187 *Selection of stranded embroidery cotton over print of slub silk.*

188 *Detail of spiral in running stitch on slub silk.*

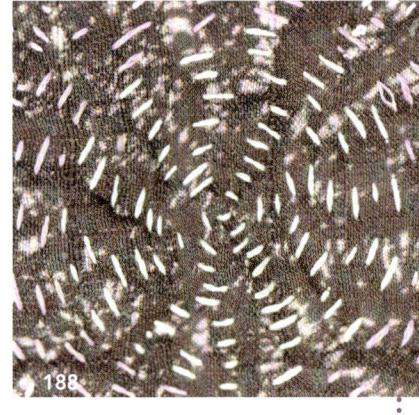

189 Close-up details showing the running stitch.

190 Reverse of throw showing coloured threads on cashmere and wool layer.

191 Cushion and throws.

192 Finished throw.

193 Finished cushions.

Deconstructing: taking a surface and disrupting it

7

Changing surfaces

While the projects in this book predominantly feature traditional hand techniques that we have contemporised through aesthetics, styling, product choice and ultimately by design, what constitutes embroidery as a wider subject of study has undergone major expansions in interpretation. Embroidery has traditionally focused on the stitch that is on top of a surface, but there are also techniques which manipulate the surface, changing its appearance, structure and handle. In fact, the study of contemporary embroidery has moved and exploited techniques that do not involve stitching at all, yet still the manipulation of the ground/surface constitutes the subject of contemporary embroidery.

With textiles we often appropriate tools that have traditionally had another use. Working from black-and-white drawings in a pointillist style is all about composition, rhythm and mark-making. Pyrography or wood-burning has seen the potential of using a soldering iron as a drawing tool. On cloth there are added possibilities as the base cloth may be thermo-plastic, where the heat forms a permanent shape, or with certain materials there may be singeing, bubbling or crystallising textures.

Making holes with a soldering iron

A soldering iron is a hand tool used in soldering. It supplies heat to melt solder so that it can flow into the joint between two pieces of metal. A soldering iron is composed of a heated metal tip and an insulated handle. Heating can be produced by passing an electric current through a resistive heating element.

194

194 *Soldering iron*.

DECONSTRUCTING: TAKING A SURFACE AND DISRUPTING IT

Manipulation of surfaces is a very creative area to work in, as there are no given rules, but what is significant is the importance of understanding and knowing the properties and potential of any given materials to exploit them by changing and upcycling them into something different from the original.

In this project the soldering iron is used to create marks, yet mark-making by this process will have different effects and success depending on the surface worked with. It is important to know how the soldering iron burns on different surfaces/materials. Always do tests first, especially if you have never used a soldering iron before. You need to be decisive and confident in your planning and execution. As a general guide, natural fabrics such as wool, cotton, silk and linen will react to burning as paper does: scorched edges with ash. If you want the scorched look, then natural fabrics are better. Plastics and synthetic fabrics will melt, with hardened, blackened edges. They also burn quickly, so you have to work very fast and purposefully. The one major drawback of working with a soldering iron is that, unlike working with paint or pencil or even machine embroidery, there is no easy way to change or correct mistakes.

195 *Manipulated photograph looking at tone and shape.*

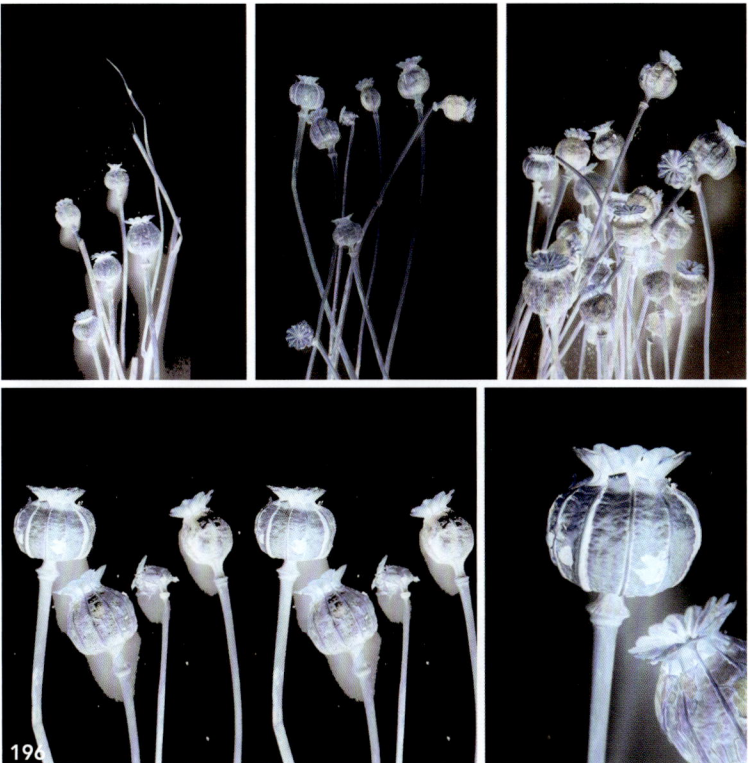

196 *Layout and composition of dried seed-head images.*

TEXTILE SURFACE MANIPULATION

Soldering irons vary in price but there is no need for great expense. What you might consider is whether you want to use a fine stiletto point or a squarer chisel end. For this project a stiletto point was used.

Project 11. Window treatment

For this project the imagery came from drawings on paper, laid under the frame. The success of the project depends on the quality of the drawing. We worked from several detailed drawings of dried seed heads. A great deal of time was spent trying out different approaches to layout and composition. Consider your needs. The fabric used in this project is an existing roller blind. This makes life easier, as you don't need to insert the fabric into the roller blind mechanism, but it means you need space to work. A blind may be a semi-permanent feature at a window, or used as a room divider, rather than being rolled up and down regularly. This blind is a synthetic fabric, but it has a loose weave. Initial sampling showed that burning long lines would have made the fabric very unstable. Small holes worked far more successfully. This was taken on board as part of the design process.

The window blind comes in a number of standard sizes. You need to consider the window where this blind will be used: does it need small repeat details or a very dramatic large image? Not all fabrics can be drawn on and if they can be, you certainly do not want to see any residue of sketches, so great care must be taken if the design is to be drawn onto the blind first.

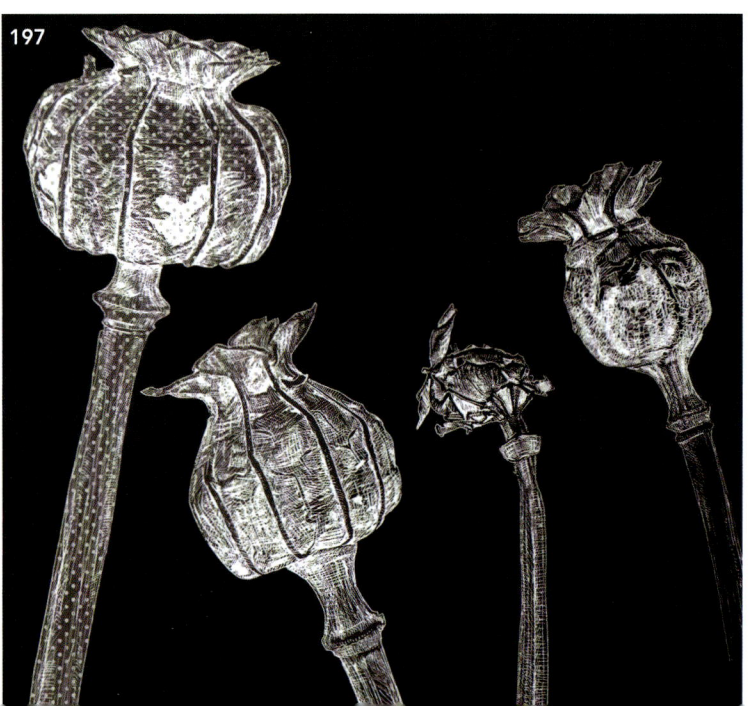
197

▶ HANDLE WITH CARE

It would be remiss of us to go any further without pointing out Health and Safety issues.

1. Soldering irons are very hot: you should never test to see if a soldering iron is on or hot enough by touching it. Do this on the surface of your swatch.

2. You must prepare a work space that is well ventilated (a garden shed or garage is ideal). Do not work in rooms where other activities are happening.

3. You must prepare a work space where the soldering iron is on a stand that will not touch any furniture tops; do not set on a cluttered worktop.

4. Prepare a frame to stretch the fabric area to be worked on, raised above the table top so as not to mark or destroy worktops.

5. If working with plastics or synthetic fabrics, burning will give off a lot of fumes, so if you have any chest complaints we do not recommend working this technique. Work in a well-ventilated room (not a family room), or even outside. The use of a mask is advisable.

DECONSTRUCTING: TAKING A SURFACE AND DISRUPTING IT

Using dots in a pointillist style means we have better control over the image. The depiction of tone and sense of form are achieved by regulating size of hole and density achieved by the spaces between the holes.

As an alternative to mark-making by burning holes, you could consider cut-work. Depending on the base fabrics like plastic or blackout blinds, you can cut shapes (always using either a sharp new blade or very sharp scissors with a good point). The sample shown (see image 205) has layered up transparent fabrics with machine appliquéd shapes (creating solid shapes in front of a light source) and a layer of cut-work shapes. The edging has been machine embroidered over a fine cord to make the fabric less likely to fray; this technique also gives a cleaner, sharper edge. The cut-out process could work on curtains or blinds, with layers adding tones and overlaps of motifs.

197 and 198 Layout and composition of dried seed-head images.

199 Inspired by the hole-punching on traditional brogues, an example of marks made by a soldering iron on a white plastic vacuum-formed shoe form.

200 Border idea using marks made by soldering iron.

201 If the holes are too close or form a line, the pattern will make the fabric unstable and rip.

202 Examples of marks made by soldering iron working in the negative space.

203 Finished window treatment.

204 Window treatment detail.

205 Window treatment detail, layered transparent grounds appliquéd motifs, top layer of cut-out work.

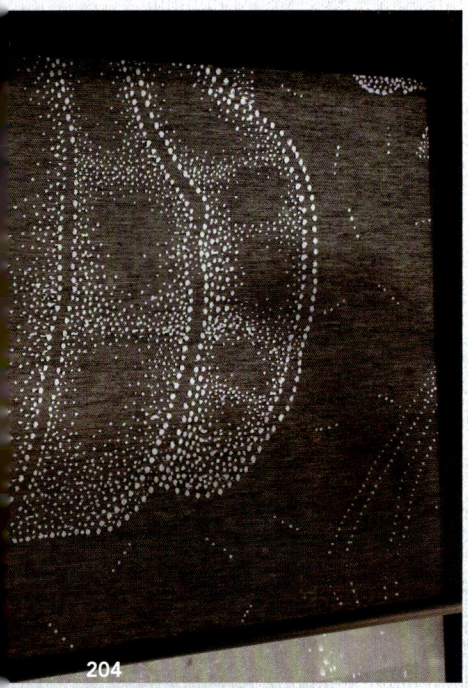

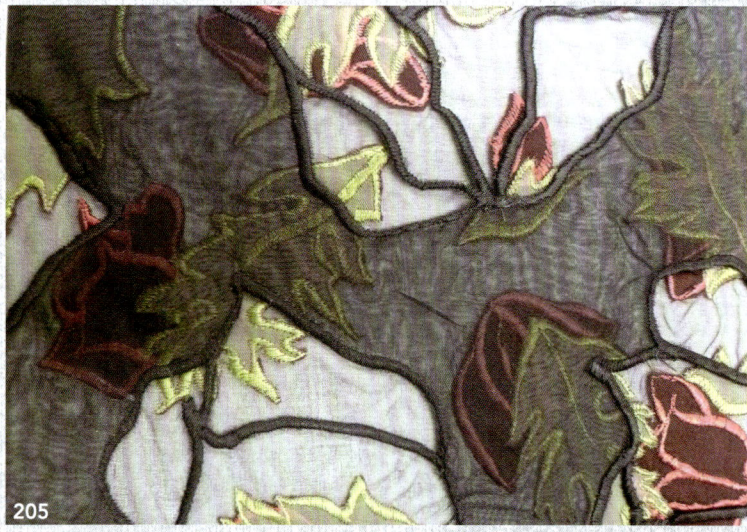

DECONSTRUCTING: TAKING A SURFACE AND DISRUPTING IT

Distressing fabrics using an embellisher machine (electronic needle-felt)

Felting is traditionally a process that produces a non-woven cloth by pressing, matting and condensing woollen fibres. It often uses a wet felting method, where hot water and agitation in the form of beating, kneading or pressing cause the fibres to bind together. Felt ranges from incredibly delicate and wispy, to a medium-weight fabric we use for children's craft projects, through to thick and tough fabrics used as construction materials.

Needle-felting is a craft process of producing felt using friction instead of water. It uses the barbed needles that were developed for industrial felting, and can be worked with individual needles or small groups of needles. In recent years the embellisher machine has been invented as a mechanical way of using the hand needle-felt technique. We use the Janome FM725, but there are numerous other machines on the market.

Needle-felt machines

These machines look like a regular domestic sewing machine. Unlike the standard rotary hook machines, they have no bobbin, just a number of barbed felting needles that are driven up and down, controlled by a standard foot control. They provide a much quicker way to needle-felt almost as a kind of drawing, laminating fabrics together, fraying or distressing a fabric, or applying a patch or appliqué. It is easy to use: simply put the fabric under the needle, press the foot control and away you go. There are no threads or bobbins, just the barbed needles. For safety it has a needle guard, which makes it difficult to catch your fingers. This is important as the barbed needles would cause a horrific injury.

You can work with a single needle, which is obviously much slower but gives greater accuracy, especially in drawing techniques. There is also a separate 5-needle unit, which can be a fixed unit where the whole unit must be replaced if a needle breaks, or an interchangeable unit where you can change each individual needle if it breaks.

Although this technique is often worked with a number of layers and fuses them together, it is important to remember that it is a destructive process: the barbed needles that puncture the fabric make holes.

206 Top *The Janome FM725*. Bottom *Working a sample, holding the fabric taut with both hands and making gentle movements.*

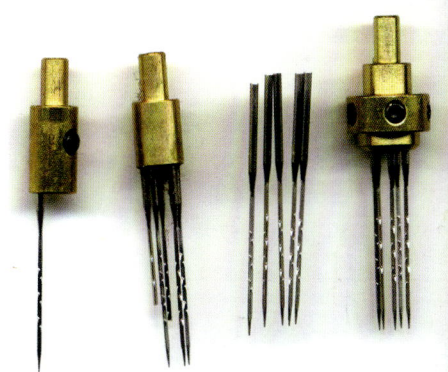

207 Left to right *Single needle; fixed unit with broken needles; replacement needles; unit with individual needles.*

103

TEXTILE SURFACE MANIPULATION

Some machines come with a single needle or a holder of multiple needles in a fixed mount. If possible, try to get hold of an interchangeable multiple holder that has replaceable needles. It's often possible to source these needles separately and more cheaply. If you plan to work on this machine in any depth you will get through quite a few needles!

Note that when one of the needles in the multi-needle breaks it can cause a different kind of mark, particularly in finer fabrics.

Seams

The embellisher is essentially destructive, however if used carefully it can join edges. This is often easier if you add an additional strip, layer or binding. There are endless ways to explore seam details. Inserting a fancy knitted ribbon between the two raw edges, then using the embellisher to fuse them together, can create an alternative to a classic piped seam. If the fabrics are slippery or if there are several layers, it may be easier to hold the edges together with a line of tacking. You could also use a contrasting thread and oversew the edge. Working this seam right side out will ensure that we see the detail in the final piece.

Drawing

It is tempting to let the machine work away and just cover entire surfaces. However, we can be more sensitive and use this as a tool to draw with. It will never give you a very detailed line; think of it more like the mark you could achieve with a half-inch house-painting brush on blotting paper.

In image 210, the back of the sample shows how the felt shape has been embellished onto the knit. On the face side of the knit we can see how the felt has been pushed through from the back to create a mottled texture.

> ▶ **HELPFUL TIPS**
> Move fabrics slowly and smoothly. Staying too long in one place will just make a hole and the fibres may pull into the machine. Jerky movements are always risky as they pull the fabric while the barbs are in the cloth and cause the needles to break. Remember: it is far better to build slowly.
>
> If you are working with fabrics of different weights, remember that it takes a lot to push a heavy fabric through a fine one, but a fine fabric may disintegrate to nothing when pushed through a heavier fabric.

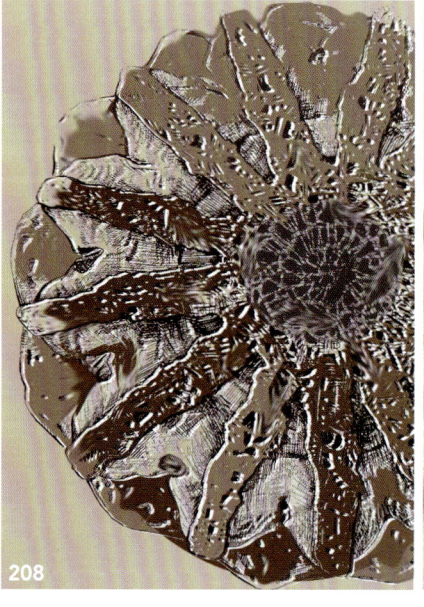

208

208 Left *Manipulated drawing.* Right *Drawing with single needle.*

209 Development from sampling ideas exploring how motifs from the Arctic poppy could be applied as design ideas for scarves.

210 Left *Back of sample, showing how the simple felt shape with snipped-out shapes has been embellished onto the knit.* Right *The face side of the knit, showing how the felt has been pushed through from the back to draw a mottled texture.*

211 Arctic poppy motif built up from felt shapes.

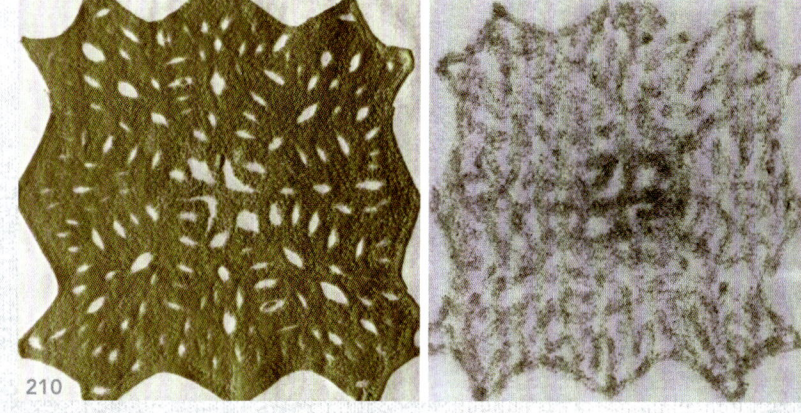

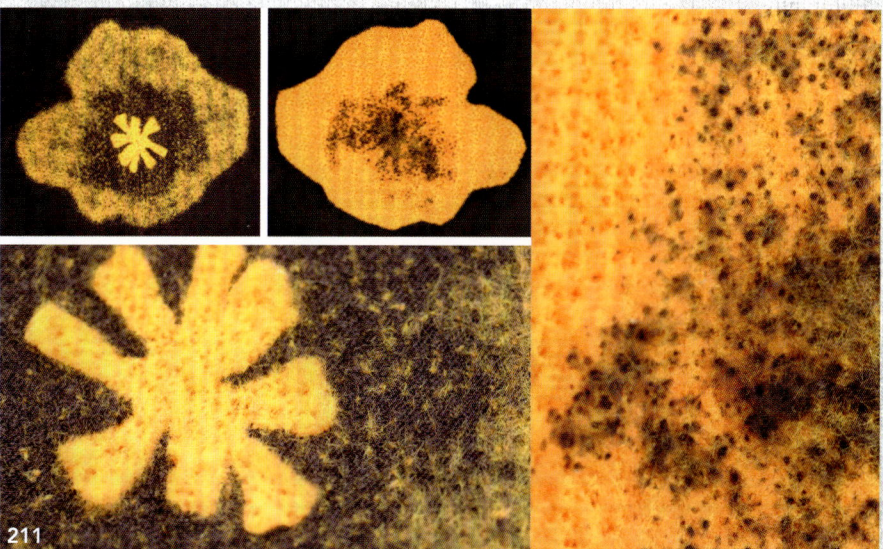

TEXTILE SURFACE MANIPULATION

An existing polka-dot print has been embellished with applied squares. The central 'beads' are long neon plastic fishing floats.

Blending surfaces

From decaying leaf bristles to dried and cracked seed heads, poppies provide some wonderful textures. Always sample with your materials before committing to a project. Sample and experiment by working fabrics from different sides and also by working in reverse. If you want them to fuse more solidly, then work alternately from both sides. To produce a tonal gradation from light to dark, work with contrasting tones. Try working from the back with a soft fabric like felt and embellish the whole surface lightly, then work over smaller sections each time so that when you reach the other end the fabric is totally embellished. Fibres like cotton are more brittle and will snap rather than fuse. Bear this in mind when choosing which fabrics to combine.

212 *Sample of embellished surfaces punctuated with plastic fishing floats as an alternative bead.*

213 Left *Photo of dried leaf with bristles.* Right *Variety of embellished surfaces.*

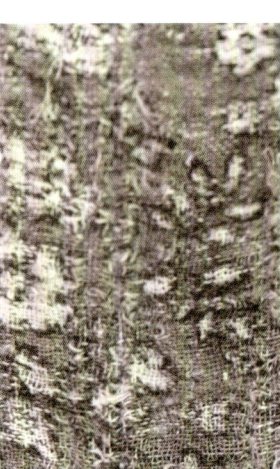

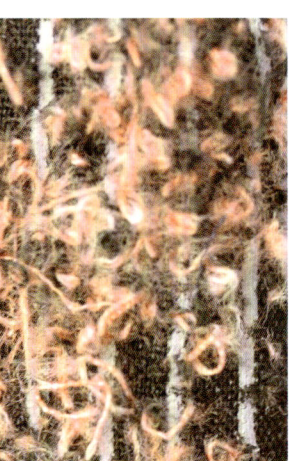

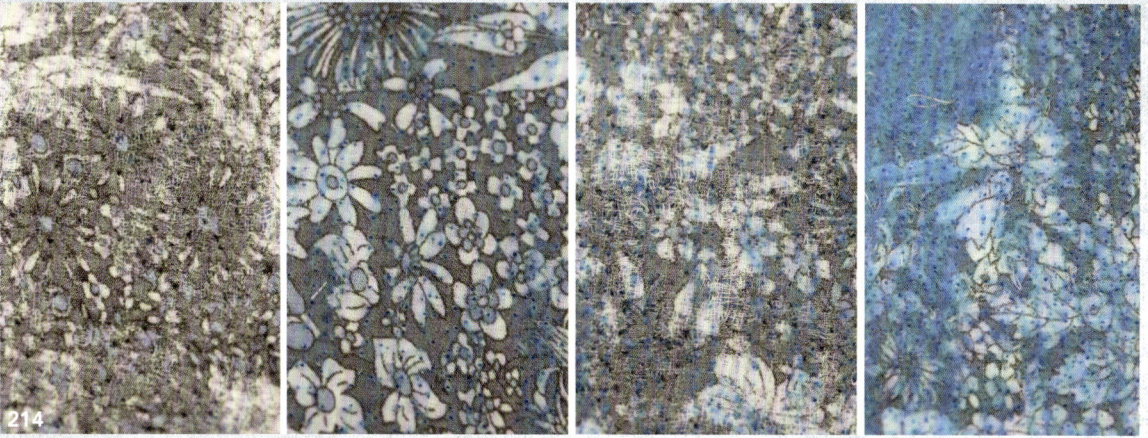

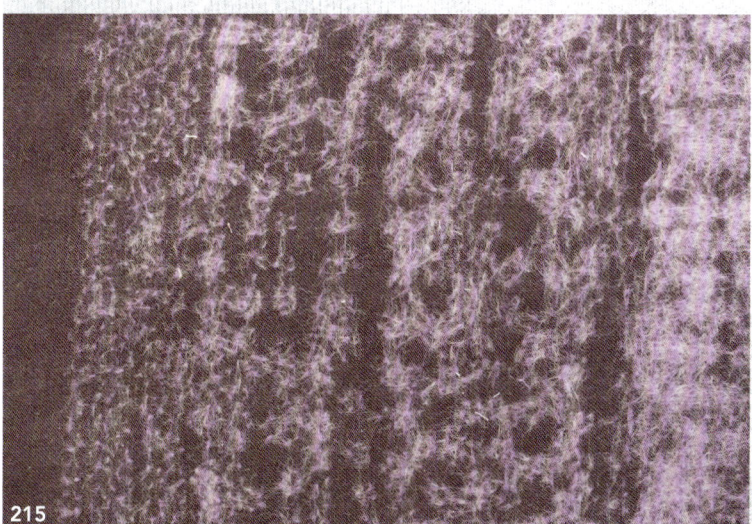

214 Left to right *Embellished from front only, back only, back then front, front then back.*

215 *Sample showing gradation by working the embellisher an increasing number of times over the fabric.*

216 *Close-up of printed polka-dot cotton fabric showing wool fibres embellished from the back.*

217 *Close-up showing the disruption of a printed fabric with embellisher.*

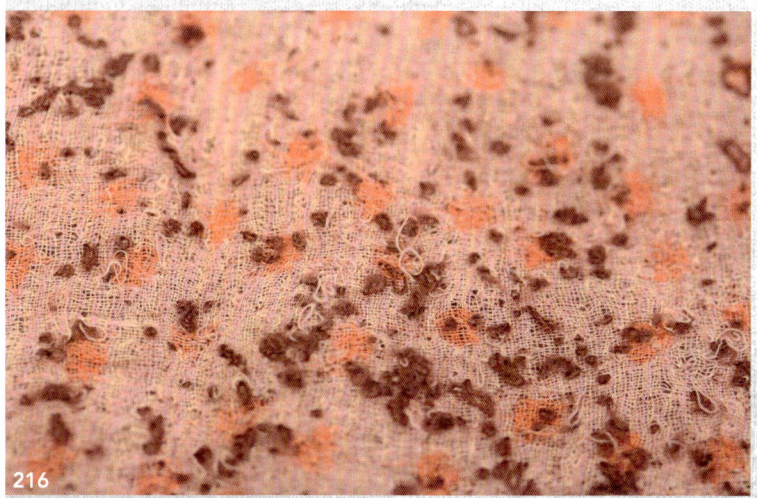

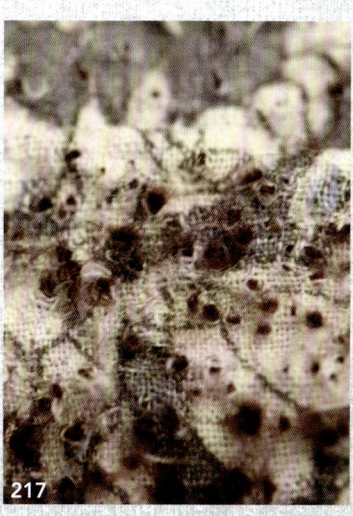

TEXTILE SURFACE MANIPULATION

218 A number of seam details. Inserting knitted ribbon between the two raw edges and using the embellisher to fuse them together.

219 The pieced fancy yarn embellished onto knit, showing front and reverse. The ribbon yarn is pieced to create an eel skin effect.

220 The same printed polyester sheer fabric with three different colours of felt embellished from reverse.

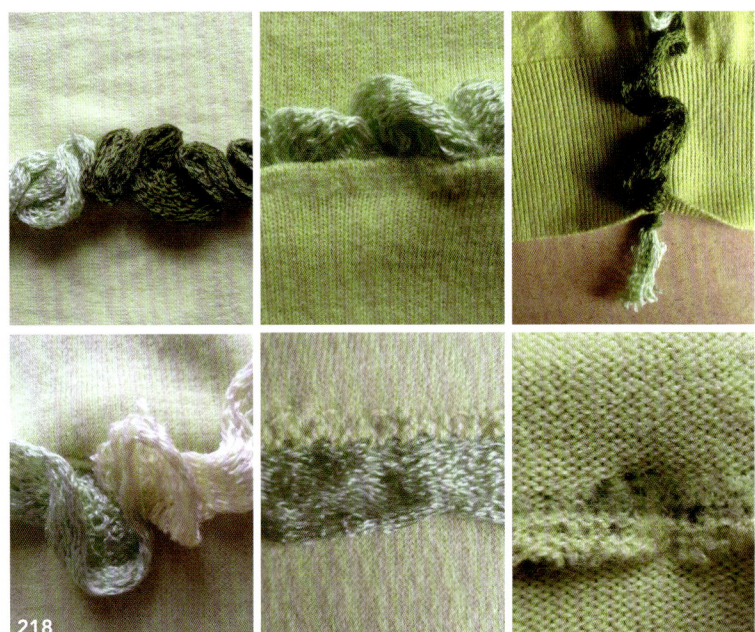

As you can see from image 220, if we work on the same printed polyester sheer fabric with three different colours of felt and embellish from the reverse, we can create washes of colour.

108

DECONSTRUCTING: TAKING A SURFACE AND DISRUPTING IT

Project 12. Scarves

Due to the tactile nature of the embellished surface (and its delicacy) this technique makes perfect scarves and shawls. Working with a lightweight, loosely woven printed summer shawl as the top layer and a pashmina-style scarf, we can see how much the layers fuse together to create a much more sturdy fabric.

These shawls are delicate and may be more suitable as throws where the requirement is for something more decorative than functional. If you work with natural fibres, you may be able to wash and felt the piece for a more permanent effect. The Arctic poppy provides an interesting motif and colour palette for alternative scarf ideas.

221 Top *Scarf front*. Bottom *Scarf reverse*.

222 *Scarf formed into a poncho where one arm is exposed. Photography by Philip White. Model: Polina Yakobson.*

223 *Detail of embellished scarf working fancy knitting ribbon over a lightweight woven scarf.*

109

TEXTILE SURFACE MANIPULATION

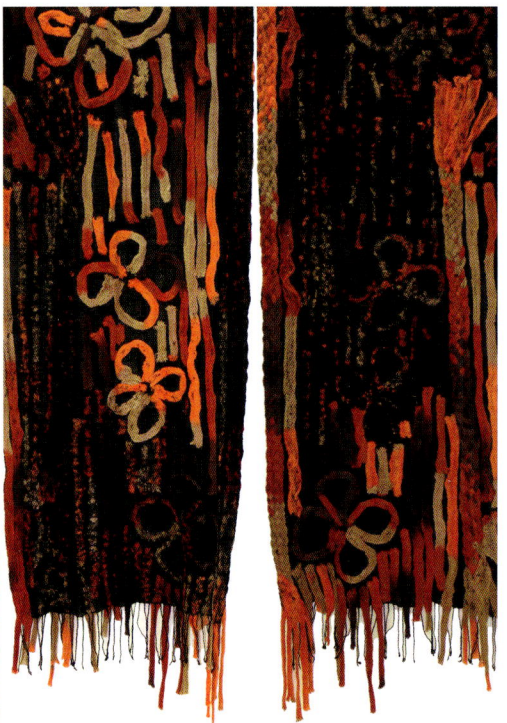

Working with a lightweight wool scarf as the base, we can apply a more dense dip-dyed knitting yarn. This creates interesting movement as the unworked areas contrast with the broad brush marks of the strip of knitting yarn. Working from the front, the yarn is pushed through to the back in a mottled marl effect. The scarf is worked with strips applied from both sides so that there is a variety of colour weighting. For added emphasis we have plaited some of the yarns to create more of a stalk effect, while in other areas we have applied the yarn to create a naïve, stylised flower shape.

224 *Sketchbook page detail showing how scarf falls when tied and the differences between front and back of reversible scarf.*

225 *Finished scarf. Photography by Philip White. Model: Polina Yakobson.*

Project 13. Upcycled sweater dresses

Charity shops always have a large array of knitwear, which may be slightly worn or damaged. The challenge here was to take parts of these jumpers and reconstruct them to create a sweater dress. You can see from the various solutions for this project that the embellisher can be used both for construction and for decorative drawing. As we see from image 219, we can use the ribbon to create an eel skin effect where lengths of ribbon are joined with oversewing and then stretched out flat and applied to the jumper. As a design feature we can juxtapose the bottom of one jumper with the top of another.

DECONSTRUCTING: TAKING A SURFACE AND DISRUPTING IT

Sketchbooks are a vital part of the design process, particularly when the material we have to work with is limited. By drawing diagrams of the garment laid out flat, we have a template with which to explore possible decorations and details. This ensures we have explored the ideas more quickly, without having to work through each idea to find the most successful solution. All materials react differently under the embellisher and a sheer jacquard-weave scarf will practically disintegrate when worked onto jersey. We can play with this process and apply it over seams and edges.

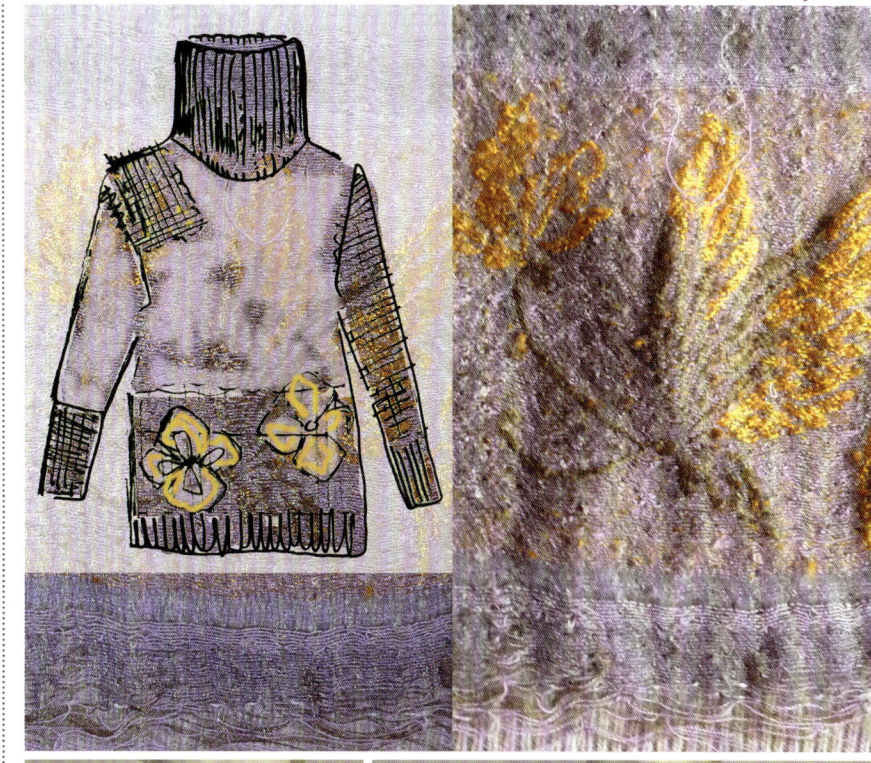

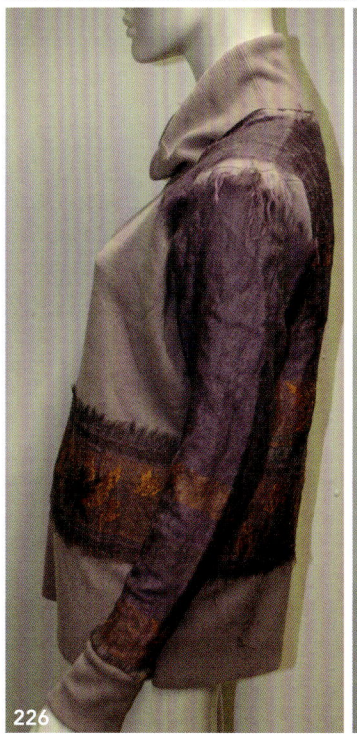

226 *Sketchbook page showing embellishing a sheer jacquard-weave scarf onto jersey over seams and edges.*

111

TEXTILE SURFACE MANIPULATION

227

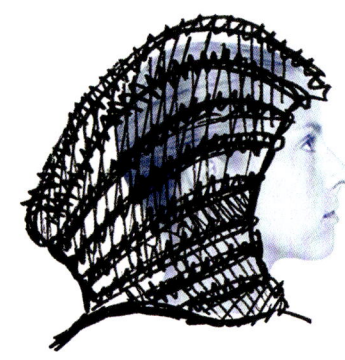

228

One design feature we have focused on for these sweater dresses is a sculptural hood. Working from the seed head as a form and the ridges of the compound pistil, it is possible to generate endless shapes. As an approach to illustration we have used an image of a face and filled a design sheet with a number of these images as a base to draw over. This ensures that we see the scale of the idea and the relationship between the head and the design idea. Even though you are working on the flat, it is important to consider how the hood will be worn and how it will be made.

To complement this we explored fusing the knitting ribbon onto a belt.

Most knitting suppliers stock fancy scarf yarns made from complex knotted structures. When knitted, these create ruffles and frills. However, the yarn itself is particularly exciting when opened out and its use reconsidered: when we insert it into a seam it creates a frill.

227 *Sketchbook page brainstorming sculptural shapes of constructed hoods.*

228 *Sketch of hood constructed from strips of jersey.*

229 *Hood samples with knitting ribbon inserted in seams.*

230 *Sketchbook looking at jumper with reversible belt.*

229

230

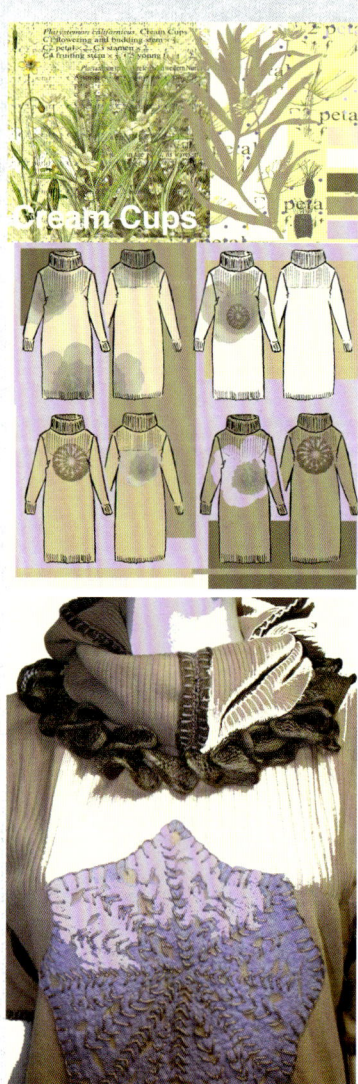

Cream Cups

Devil's Fig, Golden
B2 style × 4.
B3 fruiting stem
B4 top view of fruit × 2
B5 seed × 8.

231

232

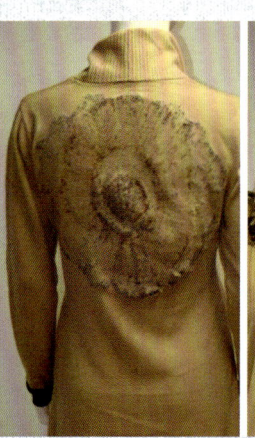

233

DECONSTRUCTING: TAKING A SURFACE AND DISRUPTING IT

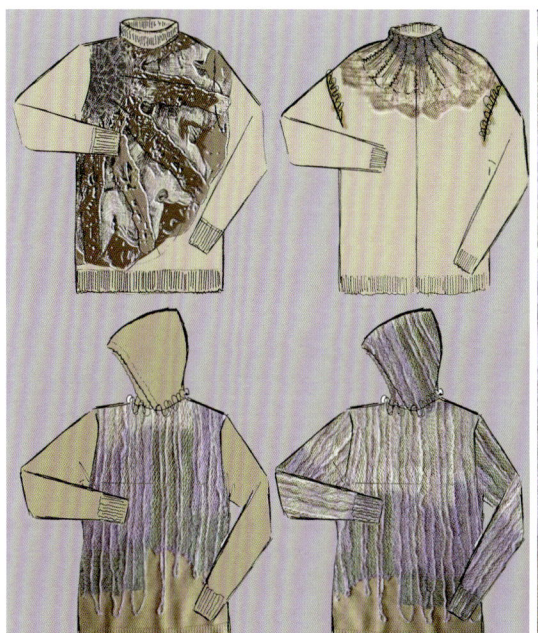

231 *Sketchbook pages showing placement garment ideas.*

232 *Sketchbook page showing placement appliqué felt with hand fly stitch.*

233 *Sketchbook page showing sweater dress idea development.*

234 *Detail of cowl neck.*

235 *Development page showing ribbon stretched out flat and embellished.*

Using a different jumper, we have explored a different emphasis with an extended turtle neck. We have also looked at how we can embellish raw edges with a knitting thread as a binding.

Using a sketchbook we documented the consideration of an appliqué placement of felt, decorated with simple hand stitch.

115

TEXTILE SURFACE MANIPULATION

Project 14. Men's jumpers

Merino or cashmere jumpers are lovely to wear, but can deteriorate or become damaged very easily. If your sweater has tiny moth holes, then why not make this a feature?

Embellishing will exaggerate these holes, but it will also felt the edges so they don't unravel any more. It is vital to consider composition and placement.

The juxtaposition of a punk aesthetic with a classic item can be fun, especially on a larger jumper that can be shaped to create a more edgy style. For a more dramatic contrast, two jumpers of the same colour but different tones could be layered together.

For this project we have worked over a fine-gauge jumper in a wool/cashmere mix. First, cut small v-shaped nicks with a pair of scissors. Place panels cut from another jumper underneath and embellish the two together. Remember: if you work from the right side you will have a subtler textured effect, while if you work from the wrong side the colour will come through to the right side.

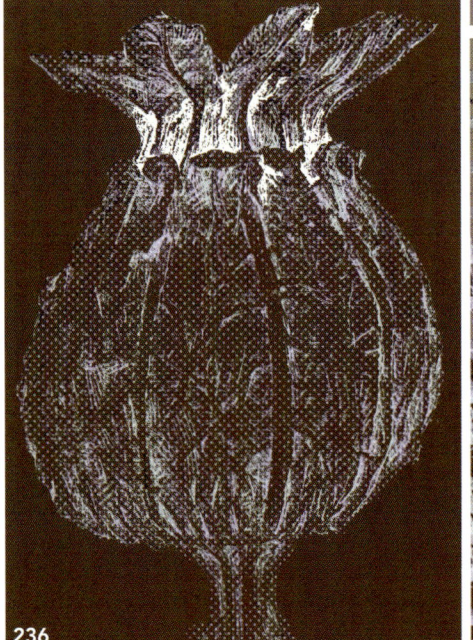 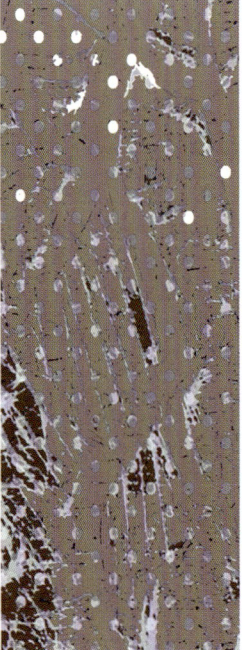 

236 Left and middle *CAD-manipulated drawing surfaces.* Right *Detail of the perforation technique worked on cotton shirting fabric. Repeated washing encourages the fraying texture. These surfaces can be applied onto knitwear.*

237 Design inspiration from the perforations in the seed head and the spots formed by the seeds themselves.

238 Men's jumper development.

239 Detail of embellished jumper.

TEXTILE SURFACE MANIPULATION

Project 15. Men's shirts

Plain cotton men's shirts also provide great scope for the embellisher.

The scattering of poppy seeds has led to the use of polka dots as a fashionable design signature for the collection. These can be interpreted in beading, hand stitches, or even print. Generating a simple single spot pattern and using automatic fills, we can create rich digital designs. The shirts themselves could be used to apply pattern or digital print, perhaps from an old scarf or from digitally printed fabrics.

Working over seams presents a few logistical challenges, so you may need to work on a larger size so that you can open up the side seams and then take them in a little when you rejoin them.

Once you have sampled and become familiar with the issues surrounding customising a shirt, it is a case of back to the drawing board! Working from technical drawings or 'flats', we can keep exploring composition and layout. For the final project we settled on a classic navy and white spotted shirt and used very subtle embellishment in key places.

The idea can be extended by exploring a coordinating scarf.

240 *Initial shirt ideas, showing distribution of colour and pattern as evolved from working drawings by fashion designer, Gareth Moloney.*

241 *Left CAD-manipulated drawing surfaces. Middle Sample with felt layered under shirt. Right Detail of shirt.*

242 *Initial idea of placement print from scattered withered petals.*

243 *Sketchbook page exploring placement of texture details.*

244 *Detail showing shirt embellishment of polka dot on polka dot.*

245 *Scarf and shirt.*

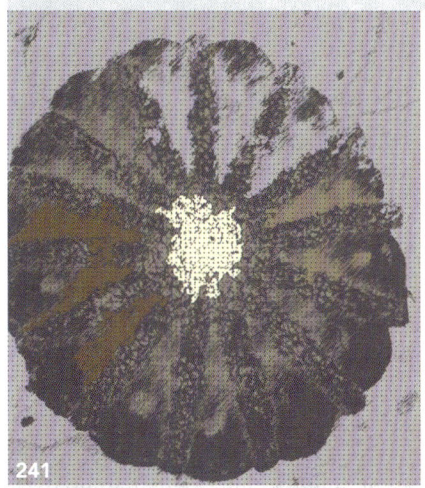
241

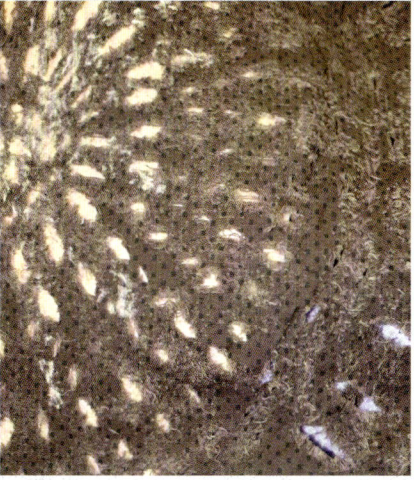

242

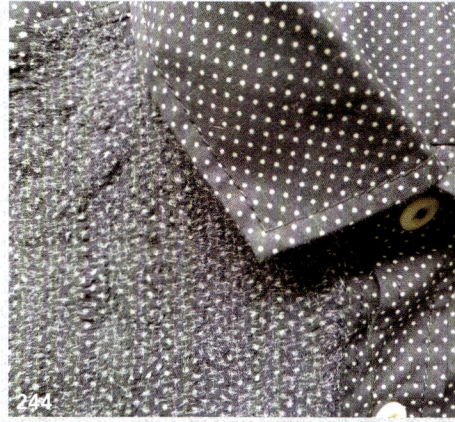
244

243

245

Trims and edges

8

Within this section we have developed a number of varied projects where beaded and embellished tassels decorate an existing accessory. These projects span fashion and interiors and show how changing the scale, colour and material of a tassel can have a multitude of applications.

By examining in detail the places where one part of the poppy joins another, such as the pistil and seed pod, we can get a multitude of design ideas for edges, seams and joins. Vintage textiles can also be informative.

Finding new design potential within the source material can sometimes be as simple as looking from another angle. Inspiration can come from looking at an inverted poppy. When looking at a poppy more closely, we see the multitude of spiky stamens that can be the inspiration for decorative forms such as tassels. Different species have different proportions of seed heads.

246 *Various trims and edges worked in buttonhole stitch.*

247 Top *Edge of poppy.* Middle *Vintage sample of picot edge.* Bottom *Beaded edge.*

TRIMS AND EDGES

248 Top *Inspiration: stamens around seed head.* Bottom *Translation: close-up of three-dimensional beaded edge.*

249 *Edging to jacket.*

250 *Machine embroidery and beaded edging.*

Tassels

Tassels are a lovely rich addition to accessories and interiors. Tassel-making is also known as *passementerie* and is exemplified in the large tassels used as curtain tiebacks. We can also see them as decorative elements on clothing and accessories. Tassels speak luxury, as they are not only visually opulent but expensive artefacts.

In this chapter, tassels are more modest in size and in terms of materials. They add detail and individuality; they can be transformative when accessorising fashion or interiors, but tassels in themselves are lovely objects. There has been a resurgence in tassels in interior design; they may not be made of expensive threads, but by their boldness of form they are often the feature objects in a room.

TEXTILE SURFACE MANIPULATION

251

Tassels use a lot of thread. Whether small, long-tailed or voluminous, the result should not be a skimpy, bedraggled tassel.

Essentially these examples use a tightly spun, medium weight, viscose rayon thread (Madeira no.40 thread). Madeira threads are produced for machine embroidery; they are relatively strong and will not fray easily once in a tassel. Madeira has an extensive colour range; this thread quality has high lustre and shine. While this may not be the look you want, do consider lustre versus matt finish of threads. In these examples it is appropriate to have a shiny tassel sitting beside fabrics that have a matt finish. You could go for the other way round, but the golden rule is neither all shiny nor all matt: exploit the contrast.

Tassels allow you to be creative, determining your form and defining your colour palette. It is important to keep track of what and how much you use in each tassel, as it is all very well to work haphazardly until you need to make more. Colour-blending can be introduced either as a shock/stripe or highlight to a tassel, or you could have a different colour in the centre surrounded by a contrast (even a complementary colour) that is only is revealed when the tassel is being handled or in motion.

If you use a single colour for a tassel, its volume, mass and movement are enhanced by the use of lustre threads, but a hint or tint of the stock

251 *Variety of small bought tassels.*

252 *Examples of complex tassels.*

colour heightens the overall effect: an all-over strong colour can look flat. Tassels should exploit their mass and three-dimensionality.

Before starting work, make sure you have enough thread and determine whether you are working two threads at the same time. Consider whether you want a stripe of contrasting colour in the centre, at one side or all the way around the tassel. Think three-dimensionally and envisage the results in your mind's eye before you start.

The next thing to determine is the length you want your tassel to be. It is always better to produce one that is too long than too short, as you can trim it to the required length. It is vital to use a sturdy base to wrap the threads around. Something like a hard-backed book is ideal as it has an indentation at the pages, where a needle can slip under and secure all the threads together. A plastic CD cover can be a good base for a medium tassel, or for a smaller tassel an old-fashioned cassette tape box is perfect. It is important that whatever you use is rigid and slim.

Having determined your thread mix, roughly note the amount of winding of thread you do in case you need to make another. Remember: thread wound around a book will look slight until it is taken off the book.

Once the winding of your thread combinations is completed, you need to secure them with a hanging thread. This needs to be done firmly or your tassel will fall apart. Use an extra-strong thread, like a linen thread (used for shoe-making or upholstery) or at least a strong cotton yarn. At the top, slide the needle under all the wrapped threads, pull as tight as you can and knot.

Repeat this a few times to make sure all is very secure. Do not cut these threads off, as they will be used to join the tassel to a pompom or form or cords. Only when you have secured them should you attempt to slide the threads off the slim form and then cut the loop.

Now you have a tail, but not yet a tassel. Secure again by making a collar around the tassel a few centimetres below the knot. You now have a tassel. To achieve a successful and not too scrawny look, it's important not to skimp. The collar can be made in a contrasting colour or hidden under more decoration. Double-thread a needle, knot the end and slip the needle through the loop to secure it around the tassel. Wrap the thread around to create a collar, then with the needle draw the end of the thread through the centre of the collar and cut off.

252

TEXTILE SURFACE MANIPULATION

Alternatively, you could add additional detailing to this area between collar and knot. The example illustrated incorporates the collar into detached buttonholing over the top of the tassel. You can introduce individual decoration here.

Trimming

Lastly, the tassel will need a trim. This author enjoys this part, and it really is the make or break of how good your tassel looks. You need very sharp scissors: hold the threads between your first two fingers and cut along the top of the fingers. Shake out the tassel and repeat until there are no straggling threads.

There is another way to cut the end of the tassel, but this is very unorthodox! It only works on long, thin tassels, but also depends on your use of this tassel. If the tassel has a stripe of colour variation this cut can add drama and playfulness. Hold the tassel upright, and with very sharp scissors, cut upwards at a very acute angle. You need to be confident to do this and make sure the shortest threads are not too short. This cut will make the threads hang in loose curls, which can be very effective. Shake the tassel to make sure there are no straggling threads.

Using tights as a ground to bead onto

Many of the tassels or finishes in this book rely on beading over a form. The technique used here is unconventional and can be applied to many aspects of embellishing. The idea is to find a form that is appropriate to bead over, recycling the found object or upcycling the form to give it a new aesthetic. It does not matter if the form is solid or impenetrable to a needle, because we use it as a central core to provide a base for our decoration. With this technique we use tights as a new skin to stretch over the form, as this instantly gives a perfect surface to work into. Tights come in a wide range of colours and can complement or give a shot effect over a brightly coloured form, or if the form is an inappropriate colour, opaque tights can give a base colour that the form may not have. Heavy-denier tights give a strong and secure base to sew into for very fine needles and small beads.

253 *Tassel with beaded seed head. The silky tail is two-toned and uses a diagonal cut to give more movement.*

TRIMS AND EDGES

The smaller the form, the smaller the beads need to be. While beading by its very nature raises the surface, often on a 2D ground, you may want more relief or depth of field. This can be achieved by appliquéing your desired shape using a colour that is different from the base fabric but which matches the beads; this will make the beading stand out without the ground fabric showing.

Creating relief

If you want higher relief, you can use felt layers. Depending on the desired height, each layer is reduced in size ever so slightly to allow the beads to 'dome' over the form more easily. The first layer sewn to the ground fabric is the largest; it is tacked in place and the next, smaller, layer is tacked on top and so forth until the desired height has been achieved. Don't rush this process by trying to tack all the layers at once, as they will shift. The dome will not be secure enough unless each layer has been tacked using small stitches that are perpendicular to the layered edge.

The projects shown illustrate how beading around a form can simultaneously create both a surface and a manipulation.

254 Top *Papaver laciniatum*. Bottom *Translation using plastic bags to create the pompom.*

255 *Plastic-bag pompom with French knitting stem. The centre shows the fishnet tights stretched over a cork.*

256 *Gradated layers of felt pads building up high relief.*

125

TEXTILE SURFACE MANIPULATION

Pompoms

Pompoms remind us of the time-consuming process of cutting out endless cardboard discs and wrapping wool through the centre until there was no more hole to be seen. Pompom-making seems not at all an activity for children, who want to see fast results, yet it can be much quicker with pompom-makers, semi-circular plastic shapes that clip or slot together. These mean that a pompom can be made in minutes. Pompom-makers aren't commonly found; in fact this author has some that were part of a kit from childhood (hence they have a well-used look about them!).

The suggestion for the tieback project (page 129) is to make medium- to large-sized pompoms. Remember, the diameter is determined by the pompom-maker's dimensions, and the density by the amount of yarn you use. Using a lot of yarn won't make it bigger, just more solid. Pompoms rely completely on the yarns used. These examples used chunky wools, mohair, cottons, plastic bags and tights. Avoid overly fine, slippery threads, as they will consume enormous quantities and the end result will be limp. It is best to think of bulk and texture, as well as visual appeal. Dip dyeing can provide subtle colour changes. A textured yarn or a natural fibre with a 'scale' such as wool or a synthetic mohair will bind together

257 *Sketchbook page showing exploration of a variety of sample pompom techniques.*

258 *Pompom makers: three sets that are used to make pompoms of varying sizes.*

259 *Inspiration from pompom poppy* Papaver laciniatum, *where some of the petals have fallen away to reveal the seed head. Petals made from scored glove leather.*

257

TRIMS AND EDGES

and secure the form better. If working with pure wool, you can boil the pompoms afterwards to create dense felt balls. You will drastically reduce their size, affect their shape and almost certainly alter the colour, but it is something to explore. You can mix yarns, or introduce flashes of other colours and textures, in much the same way as described in the section on tassels. Whatever material you use, like tassels, pompoms need a lot of it, so ensure you have a good amount before committing to a project!

Each pompom-maker has four parts (think of an apple cut in four from the centre). You pair off the parts so that you have two halves that will fit together. Holding one semi-circle, start to wrap your yarn around it. The key is to be consistent in the wrapping, starting in the corner and working around the shape into the opposite corner, repeating back and forth until the inner semi-circle is full. Do not overwrap or you will not be able to slot the halves together. When the two halves are wrapped, pop them together. It is important to hold on to both halves, you do not want the whole thing to pop open. Using sharp scissors with a good point, cut between the two halves of the locked-together semi-circles. Still holding the halves tightly, take a very strong linen or cotton thread and wrap the thread around the cut line, pulling it as tight as you can and knotting it securely. Don't cut off the tail ends of this yarn, as it is the means by which you can attach the pompom to something else. Once the knot is secured, slide off your pompom-maker segments. The pompom needs one more finishing touch; rarely is it a perfect ball form, even with careful wrapping, so trim any uneven threads to achieve a true form.

So far we have described a dense pompom ball form, but it is possible to extend this technique to combine it with a more exciting centre motif. This is reminiscent of the exposed seed head as the blooms fade and petals drop. We see a stark contrast between the hard, bulbous form and the array of floppy petals of *Papaver laciniatum*.

If you want to introduce a separate centre to a pompom, it is best to use a larger pompom-maker. Corks are perfect because they are lightweight and easily obtained. For this process a champagne cork, or one that has a 'waist', is ideal, as it fits in the pompom without slipping out. The cork could be beaded or decorated, but this must be done before working it into the pompom. In the example shown, the cork has tights stretched over it, solid denier with green fishnet over the top. Once stretched, do not cut off the tail of the remaining material as this is a good base to secure the pompom to its stem.

TEXTILE SURFACE MANIPULATION

260

The process for pompom-making starts as described above, you need to check that your chosen cork (or other object) is smaller than the centre hole when the halves are slotted together. To include a centre form in your pompom, do not wrap to fill the central hole. These pompoms will use less yarn, therefore it is good to use something bulky like plastic bags, mohair or tights. When you have the required amount of wrapping for the two halves, trap in the cork; holding tightly, cut between the pompom-maker segments. Again it is imperative to use a strong thread to anchor the cut yarn and cork together (this is why a waist in the cork is useful). If you are still nervous that the centre form is not secure, then stitch through the whole pompom. A pompom with a centre detail opens up a lot of possibilities for many variations and potential creativity.

Stems for the pompom poppies

At this stage of the design process you may have sourced the perfect yarn for the stem, or wish to make your own from threads with the exact colour and quality you need. Many poppy stems are quite hairy, so a mohair yarn may be perfect, or you may wish to contrast the tassels or pompoms with a different material. In several of the projects pictured we have worked buttonhole stitch to link the stem with the poppy head.

261

260 Sketchbook page showing details of hanging seed head, the hairy textured stem and a sample of bud and stem.

261 Samples exploring different pompom and stem constructions using a found twisted cord and a French knitting cord. Detached buttonhole stitch is used to blend the join of stem to flower.

TRIMS AND EDGES

French knitting

Like pompoms, French knitting (sometimes known as cork or spool knitting) has connotations with childhood. In its traditional use it had limited application and minimal attraction, but we can re-visit this process and make it suit our own needs. The spools are often sold with instructions. If you need a refresher course on how to start the process, instructions can be found in good craft books or on the Internet. Many people find techniques easier to learn by observing rather than by reading instructions. If so, check out online videos of demonstrations.

The spool, knitting bobbin, or 'dolly' can often be found in children's craft kits, readily available online or at craft fairs. If you are so inclined, you can create your own from old wooden spools (though these are now a rarity themselves). For larger tubes, any hollow circle or tube where some kind of pin can be attached to the rim is possible. Whatever you use needs to be rigid and strong enough to have nails or long staples hammered into it.

For these samples we used the normal four-pinned spool. If you want larger-scale knitting, this is determined by the hole size at the centre of the spool, the number of pins at the top and the thickness of the yarn used. To achieve a solid cord, wools have been used. You may think of other purposes for French knitting, such as straps for bags or belts. The knitted tube will have differing degrees of stretch, depending on the thickness of the yarn used, therefore if it is to be used for some more rigorous use, you could thread a cotton cord into your knitting to stop it stretching.

Project 16. Tiebacks

Although you can create the whole thing from scratch, it is better to find an existing cord or tieback as a starting point to build onto. The floppy overblown petals of the poppy will make this a lush accessory for a heavy winter curtain (see images 268 and 269). The beaded centre will add jewel-like qualities to an interior (see images 264 and 265).

The oriental poppies, especially Prince of Orange, have large, dramatic floppy petals that can be recreated in a fine leather. The surface of this can be brushed, or scarred to accentuate the ridges of the petals.

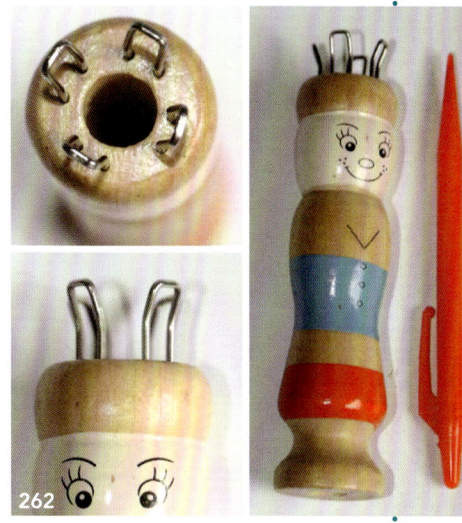

262 *French knitting 'dolly' with its four pins and hook.*

263 *Prince of Orange oriental poppy has weather-beaten petals.*

129

TEXTILE SURFACE MANIPULATION

  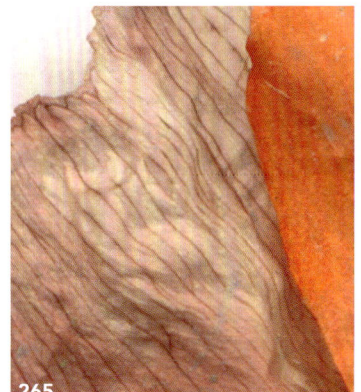 

264 *Pompom made from heavy-denier tights.*

265 Left *Decaying petal.* Right *Translation in scratched leather petals.*

266 *Small pompoms.*

267 *Sketchbook page looking at stylised poppy petal silhouette and detailed centres.*

The stylisation of shapes can be seen in this sketchbook page. If we want more layers, the collapsing petals of an opium poppy can provide a good starting point.

TRIMS AND EDGES

268 *Curtain tieback.*

269 *Detail of curtain tiebacks.*

Project 17. Wine-cooler

Simple neoprene wine coolers are available from many high-street stores. Alternatively you can make your own from neoprene or wetsuit material. If you can't find any old ones to cut up, then neoprene is available from Pointnorth mail order (see list of suppliers, page 137).

Project 18. Gloves

A beautiful pair of gloves is always a welcome present. This project shows how to decorate simple knitted gloves with tassels to make them even more special.

270 *Wine-cooler.*

271 *Knitted glove with repeat tassel border edging.*

131

TEXTILE SURFACE MANIPULATION

Alternatively, a more expensive pair of leather gloves can be turned into a sumptuous gift with the addition of poppy tassels.

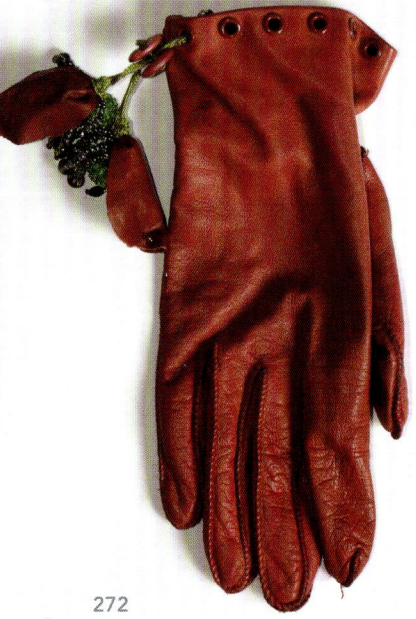

272 Leather glove with beaded tassel.

273 Detail of leather glove with tassel detail.

Project 19. Hats

Every winter the high street is full of charming knitted hats and head coverings, from the baggy 'toques' to the head-hugging 'skully' or beanie, bobble hats and balaclavas. These many styles of knitted head coverings are very popular and the various approaches to style and shape are associated with very different subcultures. For sporting events, gigs and festivals, outlandish and whimsical caps are a great statement of fun. Whatever you decide to use, try to find an object that doesn't have high-contrast multicolours, even as neutral colour as this will allow your efforts to make a statement. In the two examples shown here, grey is the base colour, so even though they are both knitted with a strong pattern and texture, the colour is a perfect foil to other colours. The knitted structure is easy to sew into and add things to. (There are no linings to remove or complicated deconstruction.) Alternatively, for those with knitting or crochet skills it's easy to find simple hat patterns and you can create your own base to decorate. This project shows how to use the pompom technique to provide details to create your own fun accessory. We advise you to make the decorative elements first and apply them in one go. It is easier to select from these than to make

TRIMS AND EDGES

274 Existing knitted hat with applied decoration. The extra-long double ties are finished off with pompoms in a variety of soft yarns. Photography by Philip White. Model: Polina Yakobson.

275 Hat with pompom details.

a bit, add a bit, and then make another bit, as this can lead to poor decision-making.

This hat had an existing same-colour pompom, a very sorry excuse for a pompom! Instead of replacing with one pompom, three have been used. If you desire a big pompom, remember that size is determined by the diameter of the pompom-maker. We have also added a chunky tassel for the top of the hat; it adds movement, connects visually to the tassels and adds to the fun effect!

The original straps have been replaced by cords of French knitting. Knit two cords to the desired length, and at the ends add more pompoms with a beading insert into pompom and tassels. The tassels are joined to the French knitting straps by using detached buttonholing around the ball top of the tassel. This not only adds a secure finish, but is also an appealing detail. If chunky wools are used for all these additions it unites the look, and also ensures that a relatively short time is needed to transform your finished product.

TEXTILE SURFACE MANIPULATION

The second example is a wide headband-style head accessory. In this example the first thing to consider is the design: is it to be a repeat pattern or overall composition? Whatever you choose to do, you need to consider that although a full circle, much of this may not be seen once worn. Plus it is important to consider whatever technique you use that it does not restrict the malleability and stretch of the knitted structure.

After design considerations and placement of motifs are decided, you can start on the padded areas for the poppy buds. These are built up to the desired height with felt layers. Sew together, cover with a fine sheer fabric (or tights). In this example the buds on the headband are disc-shaped. The reason for doing these separately is to avoid the stitching showing on the reverse of the headband. Some stitches will be visible, but try to reduce this as much as possible. The buds are then tacked on – be careful not to pull the knitting. Detached buttonhole stitch over the bud is started by first creating a tidy outline to the raised form by using small backstitch; you then buttonhole through this stitch. The premise of detached buttonhole stitch is to keep the stitches loose and open; essentially it does not attach to the raised area that the stitches will stretch over.

In this case the detached buttonhole stitch on the buds is more random. Going back and forth with irregular stitches breaks up the pattern. This example has additional full bud forms that hang off the edge. These are made of small balls of wool covered and sewn securely, and then detached buttonhole stitch is worked around the form in one direction, so the stitch pattern is more apparent. The stems are worked in chain stitch. (This is an example of a variation of the same stitch, as in both chain stitch and buttonhole stitch the needle passes through a loop of thread, the only difference is the direction of the needle coming out of the loop. With chain stitch the needle travels in the direction of the line of stitches, whereas in buttonhole stitch it is at a 90° angle.)

This stitch will go through the headband, so it is important to keep the tension the same as the band. You can add additional detached chain-stitch stems or as many buds as you desire. In this example there are flashes of orange added as detail, using cotton embroidery thread contrasting with the chunky soft wools.

276 *Headband. Photography by Philip White. Model: Polina Yakobson.*

TRIMS AND EDGES

Buttons

Anyone involved in textiles, especially in embroidery, is a hoarder, and one suspects that every coveted hoard will include a wonderful collection of buttons.

The spare-button box is most people's starting point. Every garment comes with spare buttons, though we rarely need to use them. Hence, we all have a lot of single odd buttons, lovely precious objects in their own right. Secretly we enjoy them for what they are, not necessarily feeling the need that they have to be used on anything. Just the very collection is its justification.

Buttons, though small compared to the rest of a garment, set its tone, quality and finish, they have the power to transform the mass-produced into the bespoke. Before you send old garments to recycling centres, consider the buttons: they could provide a complete set to use on something else. Use your travels to build up a stockpile; the home market may be limited. Buttons can be expensive, this has to be said to guard against the magpie in all of us that buys something just because it is a beautiful thing to have!

Although we think of buttons as functional, plastic, cheap and everyday, they have a lineage with jewellery, not only in scale but also in the materials and techniques used in their creation. Many of us buy cheap, mass-produced garments, knowing that the first thing we will do is replace the buttons with another set. The transformation is immediate.

277

277 *Collection of vintage buttons.*

278

279

278 *Button inspiration: seed heads and stalks.*

279 *Button inspiration: seed heads and stalks with initial detached buttonhole translations.*

135

TEXTILE SURFACE MANIPULATION

You may decide you want a button to read as a functioning button, or to put buttons where there were none before, in which case the closing function may be a hook and eye or snap fasteners. Coats and knitwear may have many buttons or just one large button; essentially this reads as a brooch. This can open up potential for textures and 3D forms that might be limited if we were to think of it as a fastening. Another fastening solution is that your 3D button/brooch/toggle could go through a loop made of cord or French knitting.

Project 20. Beaded poppy buttons

The embroidered buttons here are extensions of the beading projects, but they are also mostly worked in conjunction with an existing vintage button.

You could stitch images or textures on buttons. Stitch first on the flat and then stretch them into the button forms that are available in good haberdashery/craft outlets.

One tip for working over an existing button is to first go in and out of the holes of the button with a strong thread, creating a thread bar that you can then use to sew the button onto a garment. This is useful as it is likely that your embellishment will cover the holes, making it impossible to attach the button in the usual way.

280 *Button and toggle idea.*

281 *Vintage buttons with added beaded centres.*

282 *Vintage buttons decorated with a variety of beaded and detached buttonhole processes.*

281

282

Suppliers

Embellisher machines

Janome FM725
http://www.janome.co.uk/

Pleating/smocking machines

PRINCESS PLEATERS
http://www.princess-pleaters.co.uk/

Fabrics

SOHO SILKS
http://www.sohosilks.com/

THE CLOTHHOUSE
http://www.clothhouse.com/

BOROVICKS
http://www.borovickfabricsltd.co.uk/

JOEL AND SON
75–83 Church St London NW8 8EU
http://www.joelandsonfabrics.co.uk/

POINT NORTH
Hi-tech fabrics and performance fabrics
http://www.profabrics.co.uk/

WHALEYS OF BRADFORD
Fabric prepared for dyeing/printing
http://www.whaleys-bradford.ltd.uk/

PONGEES
Pre-dyed silks in wide range of colours
http://www.pongees.com/

Rubber/latex etc.

PENTONVILLE RUBBER
http://www.pentonvillerubber.co.uk/

Leather

ALMA LEATHER
12–14 Greatorex St London E1 5NF
http://www.almahome.co.uk/almaleather.htm

G.H. LEATHERS
Unit 10 Woodley's Yard
Newton Road
Higham Ferrers
Northants NN10 8HW
http://www.leathermerchants.com

Ribbons and trims

V V ROULEAUX
Trims and haberdashery
102 Marylebone Lane London W1U 2QD
http://www.vvrouleaux.com

Beads

CREATIVE BEADCRAFT
20 Beak Street London W1F 9RE
http://www.creativebeadcraft.co.uk/about-creative-beadcraft.asp

Buttons

THE BUTTON QUEEN
76 Marylebone Lane W1U 2PR
http://www.thebuttonqueen.co.uk/

TEXTILE SURFACE MANIPULATION

Haberdashery

MACCULLOCH AND WALLIS
25–26 Dering Street London W1S 1AT
http://www.macculloch-wallis.co.uk/category.aspx/haberdashery

BARNETT LAWSON TRIMMINGS LTD.
16–17 Little Portland St London W1W 8NE
http://www.bltrimmings.com/

LONDON VINTAGE FASHION TEXTILES ACCESSORIES FAIR
(every 4 to 5 weeks)
Hammersmith Town Hall King St London W6 9JU
http://www.pa-antiques.co.uk

Yarn/fibres/fleece/machine needle felt etc.

WINGHAM WOOLS
http://www.winghamwoolwork.co.uk/

TEXERE
http://www.texere-yarns.co.uk/

UPPINGHAM YARNS
http://www.wools.co.uk

Soluble fabrics, machine threads, backings etc.

MADEIRA
http://www.madeira.co.uk/

GUNOLD AND STICKMA
http://www.gs-ukdirect.com

SILKEN STRANDS
http://www.silkenstrands.co.uk/home.htm

Digital print on natural fabrics

http://www.catdigital.co.uk/
http://www.forestdigital.co.uk/
http://www.fabricprint.co.uk/

Digital print on synthetic fabrics

http://www.citrus-rain.com/

283 *'Golden Fleece'. by Helen McAllister
Photography by Helen McAllister.*

Gallery

Harmless Creatures

Are a design duo based in Dublin, Ireland. Sadhbh Doherty and Clare Geraghty combine their skills as industrial and fashion designers to tell stories through costume. They came together at the beginning of 2011 with the idea of creating the creatures from L. Frank Baum's novel *The Wonderful Wizard of Oz*. Since then they have been working on the design and manufacture of highly creative and bespoke costumes and props for the film, television, theatre and promotional industries.

Website : http://harmlesscreatures.com

284 *Harmless Creatures costume. Photography: Philip White; Makeup: Dee McKernan & Laura Rooney; Model: Gemma Geraghty.*

Dee Harte

Driven by an unfaltering devotion to knitted and crocheted cloth, she explores the relationship between subject and object. The process of engagement is a central theme of her work.

Combining reclaimed materials with intriguing patterns, she produces spatial explorations of form and function that exploit the knitted and crocheted structures' potential. Each piece is a combined response to the interaction of positive/negative space and the human connection. She employs couture finishes and intricate craftsmanship, attuned to the line and movement of the body.

Website: http://www.deeharte.com/

285 *Crochet by Dee Harte.*

Jennifer Slattery

An award-winning textile designer based in Dublin, Ireland. Having worked as a graphic designer for five years, Jennifer returned to college to study textile design at the National College of Art and Design before setting up her business in 2011. Jennifer creates textile products for the home, collections feature digitally-printed imagery and embroidery; product ranges comprise table linen – printed linen and embroidered Irish linen, cushions and throws. Collections are inspired by Jennifer's grandmother's house, where she now lives: the trinkets that link us to memories, the ornaments and objects of past generations – precious and cherished heirlooms. Jennifer's work is informed by an appreciation of heritage and what has gone before. She is attracted to authenticity – flaws, broken edges and the imperfections that exude character. Jennifer's work has been featured in Irish publications such as *Image Interiors*, *Image Fashion*, *House & Home*, *Food & Wine* magazine as well as national newspapers.

Website: http://jenniferslatterytextiles.com/

286 *Fabric and photography by Jennifer Slattery.*

TEXTILE SURFACE MANIPULATION

Aislinn Sweeney

Aislinn Sweeney studied Mixed Media Textiles at the Royal College of Art. She is a skilled embroiderer and milliner and has previously worked for John Rocha and Philip Treacy. Her talent was recognised by *Social and Personal* magazine, stating 'following in the footsteps of some of our most distinguished design exports, Aislinn Sweeney is definitely one to watch'.

She exhibited during Moscow Fashion Week (2011) in collaboration with Fabrican Ltd, producing beautifully sculpted accessories and headwear for their collection. Sweeney's involvement with Fabrican led to her making a dress for Lady Gaga.

Aislinn Sweeney's studio is in Islington, London, where she undertakes many private bespoke millinery and embroidery commissions. She also works as the International Sales, Press and Marketing Manager for bespoke furniture company PINCH - www.pinchdesign.com

Website: www.aislinnsweeney.com
Facebook: AislinnSweeneyMillinery
Twitter: Aislinn_Sweeney

287 *Corona. Photography by Joanne Warren. www.joannewarren.com*

Laura Weber

A textile designer who locates her work alongside avant-garde fashion designers who use clothing as a vehicle to communicate more conceptual ideas of identity. For her, the alliance of sight and touch is pivotal to the success of her work. She believes clothing can assist in this. Tactile sensations through surface texture and dramatic, soft sculptural forms can portray a feeling through more than two-dimensional aesthetics of colour and imagery. She strives to produce garments that speak to the wearer through the interplay of forms, structures and textures, where something like the emotions engendered by vulnerability are made physically manifest. Responding to materials and their tactility and inherent properties is a vital part of her practice. The duality of materials that have a particular look and feel is something Laura explores in the search for the alliance of the senses.

Website: ilauri-taylorseweber.com

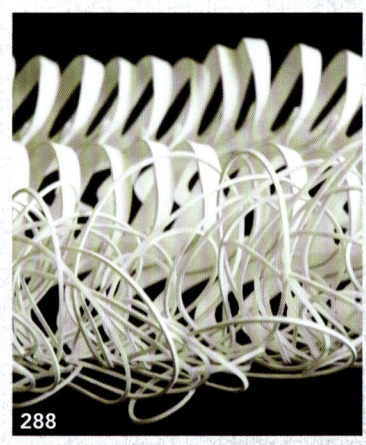

288 *Photography by Laura Weber.*

About the authors

Dr Helen McAllister

http://helenmcallister.com/

Having worked as lecturer and most recently Head of Department of Fashion and Textiles at the National College of Art and Design, Dublin, McAllister is currently the Head of Design Research at NCAD.

In 1985, Helen won a Kilkenny Travel Scholarship, which funded her first visit to Italy. Venice had a lasting and profound impact on Helen's practice. Much of her early success focused on domestic machine-embroidered wall hangings. During her postgraduate studies in 1999 her practice underwent a radical shift from 2D image-based illustrative style to 3D artefact. The work explored notions of the feminine through shoe-derived sculptures and objects inspired by the Venetian *chopine*. This work has been widely exhibited in group shows and exhibitions throughout Ireland, internationally and most notably in Venice itself.

In 2002, Helen was the inaugural winner of the prestigious Golden Fleece Award, with her embroidered shoe forms. Rooted in embroidery as a medium, her practice focuses on the exploration of hand techniques and the crafted outcome in the constant dialogue between the shoe-derived form and that of historical Venice, resulting in a practice-based PhD (NCAD, 2006). This explored the research question 'Binary oppositions – what constitutes a pair?' The work investigated notions of narrative, symbolism and metaphor that are interdisciplinary within design and that of material culture. The engagement with the viewer and the display of the made artefact propels the work into new contexts, engaging with new audiences and fuelling new lecturing situations.

289

289 *'Goldilocks' – from Goldilocks and the Bears Exhibition, Dalkey, 2011. Photography by Helen McAllister.*

290 *'Bubblegum Pavements, Dublin'. Selected to represent textiles on one of a series of stamps produced by An Post to commemorate the Irish Year of Craft, 2011. Photography by Helen McAllister.*

291 *'Venetian Water'. Detail. Photography by Logan McLain.*

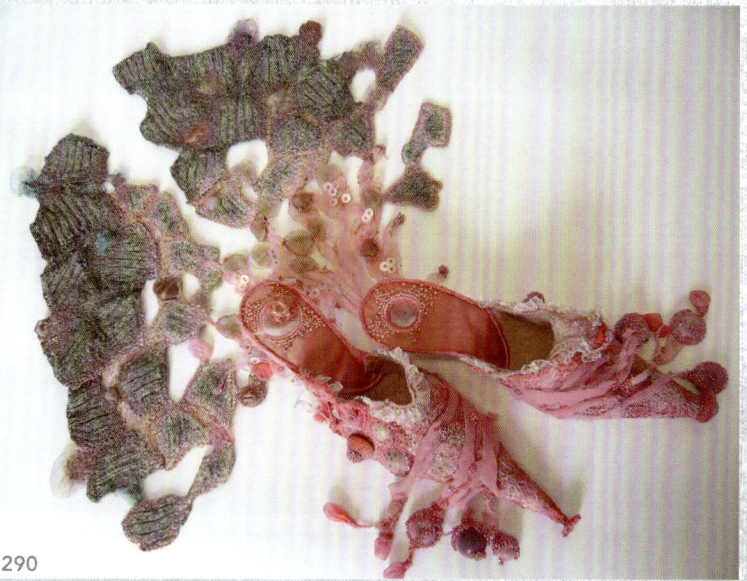

TEXTILE SURFACE MANIPULATION

Nigel Cheney, BA (Hons), MA

http://nigelcheney.blogspot.co.uk/

After gaining a first-class BA in Textiles, with a Commendation in Art History, in 1990, Nigel Cheney graduated from Manchester Metropolitan University in 1991 with an MA in Textiles. He has held the position of Lecturer in Embroidered Textiles at NCAD since 1993.

Nigel has exhibited widely both in Ireland and internationally, and his work is in many private collections. In 2008 his work was purchased by the Crafts Council of Ireland for their collection and is also represented in the permanent collection at Gawthorpe Hall. He has been the Republic of Ireland Selector for the Lódz Tapestry Triennale, Poland, since 2000. He is an expert in industrial multi-head embroidery and has worked with several companies in Ireland and the UK.

His studio practice has revolved around the act of drawing, painting and the production of stitched textiles for fashion, interiors, commission and gallery work. His training in textiles has given him a fascination with colour, surface and mark-making. Textile works range form large to small scale, but all share a love of imagery, surface and colour. Natural objects such as birds, flowers and animals are studied in great depth, while his paintings explore the contrast between loose gestural grounds and detailed imagery. Employing a full palette of textile processes including digital printing, hand and machine embroidery, his work often explores ambiguous territories where childlike phrases are reinterpreted and juxtaposed to create new images.

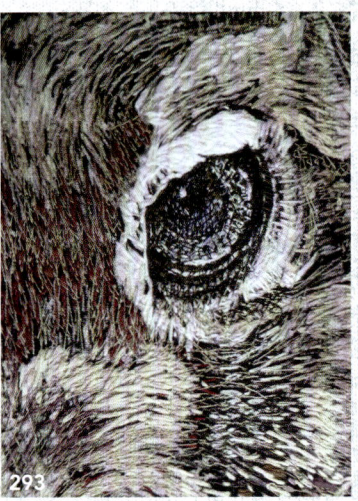

292 *Detail from large quilt 'Trinidad and Tobago', hand stitch Chihuahua image over digital print on Cotton Panama, 2011. Collection of NCAD.*

293 *'Telling Stories', detail. Hand and machine embroidered, 2010.*

294 *'2 <3 4ever', digital print, 2011.*

Acknowledgements

The authors would like to acknowledge the support of their long-suffering friends and families for their patience and understanding during the writing of this book.

We would like to thank our amazing photographer, Philip White (http://philipwhite.ie), and model Polina Yakobson. To acknowledge the support of NCAD, the Research Institute, all our colleagues in the Department of Fashion and Textiles, and in particular Claire Conway and Oongah Benner who complete team 'Art and Artefact'. A special thank you goes to our many graduates from the Design and Education faculties who have taught us invaluable lessons over the last twenty years.

Nigel would like to thank Helen for being Helen. (There is only one Helen!) Mum, Dad and Mandy for staying put in the English rain and sacrificing their usual summer holiday in the sun, while he sewed and typed. Garrett Grantham craft trims for always being the best deal in Market Harborough market for wool, threads and haberdashery. Alice Kettle for suggesting us for this project. Vanessa Edison Giles for being the best secondary-school art teacher anyone could ever wish for, and who opened the doorway to creativity, and for suggesting that he might like to look around, and stay a while? Judy Barry and Anne Morrell for creating a learning environment in Manchester Poly where all things were possible. Aunty Linda for her magical sewing that transformed some scraps of fabric into garments. Gillian Proctor for proving that we all face the same challenges and that it is a worthy battle (and that some of us can even look glamorous while doing it). To the Thorne family and my godson Orson, may he grow to be able to sew as well as he plays with dinosaurs and cars, and to Ka, Gareth, Anne, Seliena, Jaqui, Jeff, Luis, Ann, Alva and Alex for always lifting me up, however far I fall.

This book is dedicated to the fortune cookie that taught me the most valuable lesson: that 'a day without laughter is a day wasted'.

Helen would like to thank Nigel for giving her the opportunity to do what she loves to do: embroider! I thank him for giving me the opportunity to contribute to this project. Nigel continues to teach and inspire me.

Index

accessories *see* bags, gloves, shoes, scarves

bags 43–45
beading 43, 46–48, 120–121, 124, 126; *see also* sequins, fish scale sequins
bias binding 56–63
botanical research 12, 16–17, 22, 95
buttons 135–136

CAD 12, 81, 85–90, 103, 114, 117–119
canvas work *see* Rhodes stitch and tent stitch
chairs 61–62, 68–69
colour research 14, 15, 24–25, 34, 54, 65–67, 94, 105, 114–119, 130
computer-aided design *see* CAD
cords *see* detached buttonhole stitch, pompoms, tassels
cushions 62, 95–97
cutwork 102

detached buttonhole stitch 42–45, 135
differential shrinkage 82–91
digital print 6, 81, 88–90, 95–97, 117–119

embellisher *see* needle felting

felting 40–41
fish scale sequins 50–53
folds *and* folding 60–61
French knitting 129

garments *see* jackets, jumper, shirts, sweater dresses
gloves 131–132

hand stitch 6, 90–97
hats 60–61, 132–134
hoods 112
head coverings *see* hats, hoods

interior products *see* chairs, cushions, laundry baskets, throws, window treatments

jacket 53, 84–91
jumpers 111–117

kantha 90–97
knitting 33–39

laundry baskets 54–55, 67, 73–77
loops 54–59, 62–64, 74

machine embroidery 34–38, 40–41, 82
manipulation 90–3; *see also* differential shrinkage, folding, *kantha*, loops

needle felting 103–119

placement designs 12, 48
pompom 125–128, 130–133

quilting 80–97; *see also* differential shrinkage, *kantha*

repeat structures 26–32, 96
Rhodes stitch 75–77

scarves 40–41, 109–110, 112
sequins 49–53; *see also* fish scale sequins
shirts 116–119
shoes 7, 42, 78–79, 101
social responsibility 25; *see also* upcycling
soldering irons 98–102
sujini 90
surfaces *see* canvas work, differential shrinkage, hand stitch, *kantha*, knitting, machine embroidery, manipulation, needle felting, quilting, sequins, soldering iron
sweater dress *see* jumpers

tassels 121–126, 131
tent stitch 68–75
throws 95–97
tiebacks 129–131
trims 120; *see also* buttonhole stitch, buttons, tassels, tiebacks
tufts *see* folds, loops

upcycling 25, 54, 61, 68–69, 74, 110–119

vintage 43, 50–51, 56, 70
visual research 8–11, 18, 20–21, 65–66, 99–101; *see also* botanical research and colour research

water-soluble fabrics 33–36
window treatments 100–102